Women
Mentoring
Women

Women Mentoring Women

Ways to Start, Maintain, and Expand a Biblical Women's Ministry

Vickie Kraft

MOODY PRESS

CHICAGO

ISBN: 0-8024-9565-6

13 15 17 19 20 18 16 14 12

Printed in the United States of America

To all the godly women
who have encouraged me
and invested their lives in mine,
beginning with my mother

Table of Contents

Acknowledgments

This book is not the work of one woman. It is tangible evidence of what women can do when they work together in harmony and love. The 1990-91 Women's Ministries Board in Northwest Bible Church worked with dedication to host a seminar, "Building an Effective Women's Ministry." The manual they prepared for that seminar was the seed-bed for this workbook.

Hundreds of other women have my gratitude for selflessly giving of their time and energy to make the Women's Ministries program at Northwest Bible Church a blessing.

I want especially to thank Gayle Davidson, the present Heart-to-Heart coordinator, who encouraged me to complete this book and spent many hours editing and contributing to the manuscript.

Finally, Gwynne Johnson has my deep gratitude for her organizing and editing skills and for applying to this project the insight she has gained from her own experience in ministering to women.

We pray that God will use this book to encourage and enable churches to prepare Women's Ministries programs that will bring their women to spiritual maturity and equip them to serve in their church and community wherever there is a need.

Our goal is that the Lord Jesus Christ be glorified in the lives of Christian women everywhere.

Foreword

Three hundred years ago the Judeo-Christian ethic was planted and nourished in the New World. Women on the North American continent inherited an unprecedented level of freedom and dignity through the teachings of Jesus Christ. But until the mid-twentieth century, organized women's ministries were sporadic and highly restricted, largely because of lifestyle. Now, in this final decade of the century, we enjoy the most comfortable and manageable, and yet the most challenging, life of any group in history.

With the widespread decay of American morals and the increasing pace of contemporary life, women are confused. A 1989 *Wall Street Journal* survey reported that 40 percent of the women in the United States feel trapped. But the woman who knows Christ learns that it is not how troubled is the sea that determines the course of her life; rather it is the Pilot. The Lord will calm the storm, or He will allow it to rage while He calms the soul. This message must be dispersed, and God seems to be saying to His daughters, "I have removed your hindrances; now go and help your sisters."

Ministry in the New Testament sense was unknown until our Lord paused on the shore and issued an invitation to two fishermen: "Come, follow me, and I will make you fishers of men" (Matthew 4:19). When Peter and Andrew responded, Jesus began on-the-job training for the disciples, who would launch His worldwide church.

Committed followers through the centuries have continued, each one responding to that same offer, learning to let the Lord love the world through them. I remember well the day my husband and I met Vickie Kraft for coffee; she was ablaze with fervor for a ministry to women. Well known in Dallas for leadership in children's evangelism, she was studying graduate theology when she felt a keen desire surge forth to follow through on Paul's command to Titus: "Teach the older women. . . . Then they can train the younger women." Vickie and her husband, Fred, launched a new endeavor they called Titus 2:4 Ministries. From her teaching and her wise leadership has come this book, thoroughly biblical but also intensely practical.

Never has there been a graver need for women's ministries. Young baby boomers share a general chaos about self-indentity, family matters, and the issue of authority. Many printed pages line our bookstore shelves, but few are truly resource manuals for the woman who desires to follow our Lord's command to make disciples. Vickie Kraft is one who was casting her net when the Lord came by and said, "Follow me." She did, and having learned the skills of reaching women through other women, she has now translated those skills into an operable plan.

As I travel with my huband, Howard, I meet many groups of women who hurt for daughters, mothers, sisters, and friends who cannot come to terms with their womanhood. To reach out and help them, Vickie has produced a usable tool, a how-to book that also contains a clear rationale. We must understand why we act before we act to retrieve the moral fiber of our nation.

This volume is a portable gold mine. It should be installed in every American church library and a search for spiritual treasure begun. Women can do the salvage job with other women if they know how. As never before, we should be "making the most of every opportunity, because the days are evil" (Ephesians 5:16).

JEANNE HENDRICKS

Introduction

I know from experience that women minister uniquely to women. When I was a young mother of five, at a point of personal discouragement and despair, a godly older woman took a personal interest in me. Her encouragement and support at that crucial time made a dramatic difference in my life. Also, thirty-six years of teaching women the Bible has taught me many things—among them, that women have needs only other women can meet. Titus 2:3-5 understands that need and provides God's way to meet it. In 1984 my husband, Fred, and I founded Titus 2:4 Ministries, Inc., to encourage and equip women to do for each other what Scripture clearly teaches. A year later I was invited to serve as Minister to Women at Northwest Bible Church in Dallas, Texas. Fred and I realized the value of implementing a woman-to-woman ministry in a local church, and so I accepted the invitation.

The program at Northwest Bible Church is called Women's Ministries because it isn't a single program, but rather is a cluster of ministries. The core of the program is a series of Bible studies held weekly during the school year at the church and broken down into fall, winter, and spring sessions. Following the Bible study, the group disperses into a series of electives on a wide range of topics of interest to women.

Support groups have grown out of these electives and other expressed needs, and they are considered a part of the overall Women's Ministries program, although they operate somewhat independently.

Another crucial element of the program is what we call Heart-to-Heart, a program in which older, more mature women ("Seniors") are paired with the younger women ("Juniors") for a ministry of encouragement, guidance, and support. Although the entire women's program is built around the concept of women mentoring women, the concept of mentoring can be almost casually realized in the Heart-to-Heart program.

Finally, the Women's Ministries program sponsors a luncheon (or dinner) at the conclusion of the respective sessions of the all-church women's Bible studies, a Heart-to-Heart tea, retreats, and special seminar programs we call "Saturday Specials."

These have been exciting years. I have seen how creative and innovative women are. They demonstrate their love and care in ways that are distinctly feminine. They contribute enormously to the health of the local church body. I have seen women mature in their personal lives, grow deeper in their relationship with God, and develop creative and effective outreaches into the community.

Following my participation on Dr. James Dobson's radio program "Focus on the Family," women from all over the county called and asked how they might develop this ministry in their own churches. To meet that need, the 1990-91 Women's Ministries Board at Northwest Bible Church put together a seminar called "Building an Effective Women's Ministry." This book is a result of that seminar. Everything suggested in this workbook has been successfully implemented in Northwest Bible Church and in many other churches that have followed our pattern. It is my hope that these chapters will be studied by groups of women interested in developing a Women's Ministries program in their own churches. This material can be adapted by women as they develop, step by step, a program that is just right for their own church, large or small.

I believe that God's promise to provide gifted persons for the equipping of the church includes His giving gifted women to local congregations. I believe God gives each congregation the gifted women it needs to minister to the unique needs of its women. When older women train the younger women in a vital Women's Ministries program, not only are the women encouraged, but families and marriages are strengthened and stabilized.

Because the Bible must be the foundation for any effective ministry to women or men, we will first examine the biblical basis for a Women's Ministries program. Then we will provide questions for group interaction. These studies will form a solid foundation for the direction of your ministry.

Once we have presented and studied the biblical basis for a Women's Ministries program, we will survey the process needed to develop an effective one. We will discuss how to identify the specific needs of the women in your congregation, and we will show how to develop and design a program suited to your own church. In addition, we will include tips for developing and training leadership, as well as suggestions and detailed information about various programs.

Throughout the workbook we will try to deal with commonly asked questions by discussing various solutions to problems that are likely to come up. Also, we have included an explanation of the specific organizational structure we have found effective here at Northwest, along with detailed job descriptions and related advice. We have provided copies of some of our handouts and brochures for examples of format and general information.

Finally, we hope to encourage you to move ahead by sharing some feedback we have received from those who have participated in our Women's Ministries program for the past several years. More than ever, we need to provide solid biblical teaching and supportive personal relationships to women facing the challenges of godly living in a decaying society. Our experiences here and our observations from other churches have led me to conclude that a church without a vital ministry to women is like a home without a mother. This is a ministry of great importance to your church. Your women can make a difference!

PART 1
The Seed:
The Word of God

For the grass withers and the flowers fall,
but the Word of our God stands forever.
Isaiah 40:8

1
Qualified for Ministry

The Seed: The Word of God

*A*s children, many of us experienced the thrill of burying a tiny seed in a styrofoam cup and keeping daily vigil until a tentative green sprout nudged the dirt aside, unfolded, and became our own small plant. Whether it ever arrived at full maturity or not, the growing plant was reflective of whatever seed we planted: from a tomato seed, a tomato; from a flower seed, a flower; from a green bean, a bean plant. The future product was bound up in the seed. In much the same way, the end result in any women's ministry will depend largely upon the kind of planted seed, the source of our presuppositions, and our activities.

As we look to the Bible as the seed for our planting, we can confidently expect that the result will be a ministry that reflects God's character and God's view of women. Therefore, the place to begin growing your women's ministry is with a study of what the Bible teaches about women and their responsibilities before God. This study is vital for several reasons.

Tradition Versus Truth

First, we need to distinguish between tradition and biblical truth. There is a difference between tradition and Scripture. The Bible is divine and infallible; tradition is human and fallible. When tradition is based partially on Scripture and partially on culture, we must distinguish where one begins and the other ends. Discerning the impact of culture and tradition on the understanding of truth is important in planning how to implement this essential ministry to women. The seedthoughts for any effective and lasting ministry must come from the Word of God.

Biblical Calling or Cultural Pressure?

Second, social and cultural changes, such as a pervasive immorality, an increasing divorce rate, the breakdown of the extended family, and an increase in the number of mothers working outside the home, have created an atmosphere of confusion and unrest experienced by many women today, including Christian women. However, when we are pressured to develop a program centered around the needs of women in our culture, rather than beginning with what the Bible teaches, we are in danger of developing a ministry with culture-bound roots. The Bible, rightly understood and applied, will provide a program that speaks with authority and power to the needs of women.

Commands or Confusion?

Third, many women are hesitant to step into a significant role of ministry because they honestly believe it is not their place to do so. They have previously understood that the Bible places great restrictions on their ministry in the church, and they sincerely desire to be obedient to God's plan. They need the strong confidence of scriptural clarity to step out.

In this chapter we will examine the biblical basis for a woman's worth and God's place for her in ministry from the perspective of women as *qualified* for ministry. In the next chapter we will discuss women as *called* to ministry.

Qualified by Original Design

One of the first things the Bible tells us about women is that they have been created in the image of God.

> Then God said, "Let us make man in our image, in our likeness, and let them rule over the fish of the sea and the birds of the air, over the livestock, over all the earth, and over all the creatures that move along the ground."
>
> > So God created man in his own image,
> > in the image of God he created him;
> > male and female he created them.
>
> God blessed them and said to them, "Be fruitful and increase in number; fill the earth and subdue it. Rule over the fish of the sea and the birds of the air and over every living creature that moves on the ground" ... And it was so. God saw all that he had made, and it was very good. (Genesis 1:26-31)

Man and woman were created *equal in nature.* They are persons of intellect, emotions, volition, and spirit. God also assigned them joint responsibility and personal accountability. They were both given dominion; the woman was co-regent with her husband. They were mutually blessed; they both were to reproduce. Neither one could have done it alone, so it was a joint blessing.

However, although created to be *equal in nature,* they were also created *different in source and in function.* Adam was created from the dust of the ground, but the woman was created from him, from a rib taken from his side (Genesis 2:21-23). Therefore they had a different source. Their physical bodies were different, and their function in reproduction was different. Both were essential.

Not only that, but the woman is said to have a different purpose. She was created to be a "helper suitable to him." The word *helper* has often been misunderstood today. Some have taken it to mean a doormat, an inferior person. Interestingly, the Hebrew word translated "helper" (*ezer*) is used nineteen times in the Old Testament (for example, Exodus 18:4; Deuteronomy 33:7; Psalms 10:14; 33:20). Only four times is it used to speak of people helping people, peer helping peer. The other fifteen times it is used to refer to God's helping people, a superior helping an inferior. It is *never* used in any of the nineteen references of an inferior helping a superior. The term also has the meaning of someone who brings another to fulfillment.

Eve could be a "helper suitable for" Adam because she was his equal in personhood. God brought all the animals before Adam first to demonstrate that not one was there for him. He needed someone like himself. And he recognized her, exclaiming in essence, "Wow! This is now bone of my bones and flesh of my flesh." This was what he had been waiting for. She could complete him because she was his equal in personhood. Yet because Adam and Eve were different from one another, each supplied what the other one lacked.

God instituted marriage for the protection of our sexuality. Physical intimacy is one of God's richest gifts, given with love to be fully enjoyed within the protective fence of marriage, between one woman and one man. Throughout the Bible, sexuality within marriage is honored, valued, and celebrated; however, sexual relationships outside of marriage are consistently condemned. Marriage is the fence a loving God established for the protection of His people.

Man's Designer and Creator knows best how we were designed to function as His creatures. God's image is man, male and female, created equals, to be in perfect harmony with one another and with their Creator. Man and woman were to function as His representatives on earth. They were to share equally in everything: in obedience, in blessing, in ruling and subduing, in reproducing, and in fellowshipping with God in the garden.

Therefore, the first reason that woman can enjoy a sense of worth is that she was created in God's image. She is qualified for ministry through creation.

Qualified by Redemption

The second reason the Christian woman can enjoy a healthy sense of self-worth and feel confident to minister is that she was redeemed at great price. Even today, we often determine the value of an item from the price paid for it. Think of the recent sale in the millions of dollars for one painting by Picasso. How much more valuable are those who have been redeemed at the greatest price, the precious blood of Jesus Christ, the very Son of Almighty God. "For you know that it was not with perishable things such as silver or gold that you were redeemed from the empty way of life handed down to you from your forefathers, but with the precious blood of Christ, a lamb without blemish or defect" (1 Peter 1:18-19). "For Christ died for sins once for all, the righteous for the unrighteous, to bring you to God. He was put to death in the body but made alive by the Spirit" (3:18).

Galatians 3:28 tells us "there is neither Jew nor Greek, slave nor free, male nor female, for you are all one in Christ Jesus." There is equality in Christ. With Him, no superiority or inferiority based on race, social class, or gender exists.

The way of salvation is the same for man and woman. Each is a sinner. Each must personally trust Jesus Christ alone to save. Each is then forgiven, receives eternal life, becomes an adult son or daughter in God's family (Romans 8:16-17; Galatians 4:6-7), and becomes a priest with full access to God (1 Peter 2:9).

With salvation, the Holy Spirit comes to indwell each individual (1 Corinthians 6:19) and to give each one spiritual gifts without discrimination based on gender (1 Corinthians 12:7). Each person, man or woman, is responsible to live a life of dependence upon the Holy Spirit and of obedience to the Lord.

A woman is qualified and equipped by redemption.

Qualified by Old Testament Example

A third reason women are qualified for ministry is that in Scripture God uses women in key ministry for Him. Abraham's wife Sarah is given as a model to follow in relationship to our own husbands (1 Peter 3:1-6). Her respect and response to Abraham reflect godly submission. But Sarah was no doormat. She was outspoken and feisty, yet protective and supportive of Abraham. However, it is interesting to note in Genesis 21:12 that God commands Abraham to obey Sarah. Most women will admit they would enjoy having a voice from heaven say to their husbands, "Do whatever she tells you to do." That is what God did for Sarah. The same Hebrew word used for obeying God in Genesis 22:18 regarding Abraham's obedience to God is used in 21:12 concerning Abraham's obeying Sarah's words regarding Hagar.

Miriam, the sister of Moses, is called a prophetess (Exodus 15:20-21), one who speaks God's word; and in Micah 6:4 God tells Israel that he set before them as leaders Moses, Aaron, *and* Miriam. In the latter passage, Miriam is clearly called one of the leaders of Israel.

Women the Bible calls "skilled" and "willing" voluntarily contributed of their possessions and worked with their hands in constructing the Tabernacle (Exodus 35:21-22, 25-26). Women served in the doorway of the Tabernacle. The same word for service was used of them as for the Levites (Exodus 38:8; 1 Samuel 2:22).

Most of us remember Deborah as the one who commanded Barak to lead the army when he was unwilling to step forward into leadership. But she was also a judge of Israel and a prophetess as well. She lived between Ramah and Bethel in Mount Ephraim, and the children of Israel came up to her for judgment. In addition, following the great victory over Sisera, she demonstrated her poetic gift as she and Barak worshiped God in a song of praise (Judges 4–5). Her words are recorded for posterity.

Hannah was a woman of total commitment to and passion for God. She had access to God, made a vow, and kept it. Her deep faith and commitment gave Israel Samuel, a leader who turned the nation around, introduced the kingdom, and anointed Israel's first two kings (1 Samuel 9, 16).

Abigail rescued her household by demonstrating great courage and initiative. She gave David wise counsel, calling him back to himself and to God, thereby saving him from taking murderous revenge (1 Samuel 25).

After the great conviction that ensued upon the reading of the law, Josiah sent Hilkiah, the high priest, and his other officials to inquire of the Lord for him concerning what to do, since Israel had so long neglected God's word. Hilkiah went to Huldah, the prophetess, for God's directions, even though both Jeremiah and Zephaniah, also prophets of the Lord, were living in Jerusalem at the same time (2 Kings 22:11-20). It has sometimes been taught that women can only do certain jobs if there are no men available. This passage does not support that assertion.

The entire book of Esther recounts the story of a courageous young woman who risked her life and comfortable position to save her people from a murderous enemy. Her words "If I perish, I perish" are understood by all women who risk obedience to God in perplexing and difficult situations.

Proverbs 31 describes a woman who is often overwhelming to women who consider all that is written about her. Here was a priceless woman who feared God, cared for her family, managed her home, and used all her abilities and talents. She bought and sold land, manufactured and retailed textiles, and more. The scope of her activities was almost without limit. We can gain courage, however, when we consider that most likely this list covers a lifetime of effort, with no doubt different emphases in different seasons of her life. (And it is almost certain that she had servants to assist her.) Certainly we can be encouraged if we look at the freedom, authority, and scope that lay open to her. She is praised for her exemplary life, not only by her children, but by her husband as well.

Women in the Old Testament were provided for in the ceremonial, civil, and moral law. They participated in worship, art, family life, and community life with creativity, decisiveness, freedom, and authority. They used their gifts and talents to serve God and to influence their families and their nation. It is important to realize that they were never forbidden to speak in public in the Old Testament.

Qualified by the Example of Jesus

Women were prominent in the life of Jesus. Jesus obeyed Mary, His mother, as a child and respected her as an adult. Even in His agony on the cross, one of His last concerns was to provide for her care. His attitude toward women was definitely countercultural. In a day when the rabbis said they would rather teach a dog than to teach a woman and would rather burn the Torah than to teach it to a woman, Jesus taught women spiritual truth (Luke 10:38-41; John 4; 11:1-44). He spoke to women publicly (John 4) when, by contrast, a rabbi would not even speak publicly to his wife. It was women who supported Jesus from their private wealth. It is also interesting to realize that Jesus let women travel with Him during His public ministry (Matthew 27:55; Luke 8:1-3).

Although women were not considered reliable witnesses in a legal matter, Jesus considered them to be valid witnesses (Luke 24:9-11). Indeed it was to women that He gave the responsibility of being the first to testify to His resurrection. Many of Jesus' parables and illustrations contain examples with which women would particularly identify: the lost coin (15:8-10), yeast and bread (13:20), childbirth and labor (John 16:21). Jesus demonstrated unusual sensitivity and compassion toward women and performed miracles for them. He healed their sick and raised their dead to life (Luke 4:38-39; 8:40-56; 13:10-17; John 11:1-44). Rather than condemning them for even flagrant sexual sin, He forgave them and offered them new life (John 4:1-42; 8:1-11).

Mary's extravagant worship near His death was accepted by Jesus, and He defended her against the unjust criticism of the disciples (Mark 14:1-9; John 12:1-8). He guaranteed her remembrance in history for her love and generosity. His commendation, "She has done a beautiful thing to me.... She did what she could" (Mark 14:6, 8), provides insight into how God considers our talents, limitations, and opportunities when He gives us our final report card.

There is also an interesting balance between the sexes in the gospel accounts. Both Mary, Jesus' mother, and Zacharias, John the Baptist's father, have a song that is recorded. In the Temple, Simeon and Anna both welcomed the new baby. Jesus had conversations about the new birth with both Nicodemus and the Samaritan woman. Peter's confession, "You are the Christ, the Son of God, who was to come into the world" (Matthew 16:15) is balanced by Martha's similar confession in John 11:27. Both a man (Luke 6:6-10) and a woman (13:10-13) were healed in the synagogue, and, as we have said, both men and women traveled with Jesus. This amazing balance is even more striking when the culture of Jesus' day is considered.

Jesus never spoke condescendingly to women, never made derogatory jokes about women, never humiliated or exploited women. No wonder they loved Him! Moreover, women did not deny, betray, or desert Him. They were last at the cross and first at the tomb, and, after the resurrection, He appeared first to a woman, Mary Magdalene.

Qualified by the Example of the Early Church

What about women in the early church? Can we find historical precedent for a ministry by women? We can indeed. Women were present at Pentecost (Acts 2:1-4; cf. 1:12-14). Like Lydia and Priscilla, many hosted the early church meetings. There were no church buildings until the third century, and therefore all the early church meetings were conducted in homes. We can be sure that if women had not been involved, those homes would not have been available.

Women were active in ministry in the early church. In Acts alone, thirty-three women are named specifically. Priscilla was a teacher who taught Apollos. She and her husband, Aquila, were an effective team in the support and spread of the gospel. Paul calls her a "fellow worker" in Romans 16 and says that she and her husband risked their lives for him. Lydia, in Acts 16, was the first convert in Europe and hosted the church at Philippi. Dorcas was called a disciple, a helper of widows and the poor, and someone who used her homemaking skills (Acts 9). Philip's four daughters were prophetesses (12:8-9). A prophet speaks God's word. Is it reasonable to believe that Philip's daughters were given the gift of prophecy and then forbidden to speak? It wouldn't make sense.

Euodia and Syntyche were women who "contended" at Paul's side for the gospel (Philippians 4:2-3). They were very influential in the church at Philippi and had a valuable ministry with Paul, something rarely noted because the reference in Philippians deals with a difficulty between these two women.

In Romans 16 ten women are mentioned, eight by name, and others are included in general phrases, such as "the household of Stephanos." Junias (feminine gender name) was a relative of Paul's whom he called "outstanding among the apostles" (v. 7). Like Stephen, in the Greek Phoebe was called a *diakonos,* which translated means "servant," "minister," or "deacon." Furthermore, church history indicates that the early church had an order of women deacons who instructed women and prepared them for baptism. It was also recorded in Roman history that Christian women called "ministers" were imprisoned for their faith.

Phoebe is also called a *prostatis,* a Greek term meaning "patron," "protector," or "champion." This is the only place in the New Testament where this word is used. It is likely that she was like prominent Christian women today who sponsor significant projects for missions and outreach or who network to put those seeking to promote evangelism in touch with other significant people. She would pave the way with introductions.

In Romans 16 Paul refers to Mary, Tryphena, Tryphosa, and Persis in terms he does not use for the men. He states of the women that they all worked "hard in the Lord" (vv. 6, 12), an expression that in the Greek has the meaning of "toiling to the point of exhaustion."

Then Paul refers to Rufus's mother, "who has been a mother to me" (v. 13). How interesting to observe that Paul appreciated having a mother, just as anyone else. He never reached the point where he didn't enjoy having someone mother him a little.

Women were active in public worship. Often in reading 1 Corinthians 11 regarding women and head coverings, we become so involved in the headcovering and what it is supposed to be that we forget the first words of verse 5, "And every woman who prays or prophesies." These women were speaking God's word and praying in the public worship service. Women were considered qualified and were given the opportunity to minister in the early church.

Qualified by Scriptural Injunction

What about women's ministries today? In 1 Corinthians 12 we see that each woman receives spiritual gifts for the building up of the body, not just for herself. The gifts are given by the Holy Spirit as He chooses without discrimination based on gender. Take, for instance, the gift of pastoring. In the Greek, "pastor" is the word "shepherd." I believe that there is a difference between the office and the gift, and that whereas there should be male leadership in the *office* of pastor, more women have the *gift* of pastoring than men. What is pastoring? It is feeding, caring for, and nurturing the sheep, and binding their wounds. What does that sound like? Mothering!

Ephesians 4:11-12 tells us that gifted people are given to the church to prepare God's people for works of service. Therefore, women are to be prepared and are to prepare others for service. Titus 2:3-5 teaches us clearly that the leadership of the church is to delegate to older, spiritually mature women the task of teaching and training the younger women in some specific ways.

In our churches today we have a great variety of ministries that are not specifically required by Scripture. But in Scripture there is a clear command for a ministry by women to women.

Qualified by Opportunity

There is almost no limit to what women can do today. They can evangelize, teach, serve on church staffs and committees, and be administrators. They can be involved in education at every level, from preschool to graduate school; in children's and youth ministries; in music, art, and drama. They can help the poor and needy in practical ways. Most of all, women can encourage women in this complex and confused society.

Women understand women. We must teach them the Word so that they know God's standards in order to be equipped for ministry. Then we must encourage them to use their gifts to serve each other and the world around them. It is essential to have women teachers and role models for the generation following us. We must examine our beliefs and attitudes about women and be certain that they are biblical rather than traditional or cultural. Men and women need one another, and neither can serve the Lord effectively with an attitude of independence, superiority, or inferiority toward the other.

"In the Lord, however, woman is not independent of man, nor is man independent of woman."
1 Corinthians 11:11

The Scripture passages given in the boxes in this chapter should encourage you as you develop your women's ministry. Not only are you doing a job that God commands you to do, but you are doing a job He has equipped you for. He has given you the resources you need to accomplish His work. You have His indwelling Spirit, who has gifted you and will enable you. You have the acceptance and love of the Son of God demonstrated to you in the Scriptures. You will have other gifted women to work with you, sharing your vision and ministry. Knowing when you set out that it is clearly God's will to develop a ministry for women to women will give you stability, certainty, and confidence. You will be able to stand firm and press onward regardless of obstacles.

Qualified by the Blessing Their Ministry Brings to the Entire Church

Jill Briscoe has well said about the need for women to have significant ministry, "When men of God recognize the gifts of women of God, and with their blessing and under their authority, encourage their use, the church of God will be blessed."

Women, both *single and married,* are blessed by a women's ministry because it helps them to mature spiritually. This maturing will affect every part of their lives. They will grow in confidence because they will learn that their self-worth is not derived from any human being, but from God. Women working outside the home will see their employment as ministry. Single women will learn that they have value and opportunities for ministry. God loves us, as women. He will be a Father and husband to us (Psalm 68:5; Isaiah 54:5). He will give us an eternal impact as we serve Him.

The *family* is blessed as women become better wives and mothers, contented with their influential responsibility to raise the next generation. Many husbands will be encouraged by the example of their wives to become more committed to the Lord. Marriages are strengthened.

The *church* is blessed by the involvement of these gifted women. Their participation will supply many more volunteers for service in every area. The image of God is male and female. The Body of Christ is male and female. Therefore, this image should be reflected wherever possible. Women should be on the church staff, the worship committee, the missions board, the building committee, the mercies committee, the discipline committee, and the Christian education committee; and they should be involved in teaching Sunday school and club programs.

Let me share with you some comments I've received from those who serve on the Women's Ministries Board of Northwest Bible Church about the benefits they have received from the women's ministry:

- "I now have strong relationships with other women I may not have met otherwise."

- "I feel so much more a part of our church."

- "My walk with the Lord has been strengthened by the role models of more mature women."

- "The opportunity to work with other women in a true team effort has been wonderful."

- "I love being accountable to the other women on the board."

- "I've developed skills in organization, leadership, and compromise."

- "I love the creativity and the brainstorming."

- "There is such a sense of family."

- "I've learned different approaches to problems."

- "My faith has been encouraged as I've seen God answer prayer."

- "Personally, I have become much more confident in my gifts and abilities, and I feel a great sense of accomplishment in what God has enabled me to do."

- "I have become more comfortable in speaking before a group. I'm more sensitive to reaching out to newcomers and relating to people in general."

- "The fellowship among the board members and the sharing of our lives has strengthened my female identity and heightened my self-esteem and self-acceptance. I feel more comfortable about allowing my imperfections to show, to drop my mask, to make mistakes. The years have shown me in a practical way that I am important because I'm me, not just because of what I do."

Wouldn't you agree that this is an essential ministry for every church? Nothing else can accomplish what an effective ministry to women by women will do. Male leaders in the home and church should not think of themselves as prison wardens whose job it is to confine and repress women. Instead, enlightened church leadership, like a husband who lovingly leads his family, should provide an atmosphere like a greenhouse. There women can grow, blossom, and develop to their full potential with the blessing, provision, protection, and encouragement of the church leadership.

Each woman is unique—there is no one exactly like you or me in all the world. Each of us is influential in the sphere God has given to us in which to make an impact—our family, church, place of employment, friends. For that reason each of us is responsible and accountable to God for how we use the gifts and opportunities He has given us. Each of us will stand before Him individually as a woman.

This is the message I hope you will bring to the women of your church. When you can demonstrate from Scripture how God values them, and they begin to serve Him with enthusiasm and growing freedom, there is no limit to what can happen as God works through them in your congregation.

Questions for Study and Discussion

1. Read Genesis 1:26-31. What do men and women share as persons created in the image of God?

2. Reach Genesis 2:18–25; Exodus 18:4; Deuteronomy 33:7; and Psalms 10:14; 33:20. From these passages, what do you learn about the word helper as used in Genesis 2:18, 20? Were any of these thoughts new to you?

3. Read Genesis 2:21-25. When was marriage instituted? What do you think is implied by the sentence "The man and his wife were both naked, and they felt no shame"?

4. What aspects of redemption are shared by men and women?

5. Study the passages of Scripture that deal with some of the women discussed in this chapter who were used by God in the Old Testament. What were some of their leadership characteristics? Which characteristics would you ask God to develop in you?

6. What lessons from the life of Jesus impressed you regarding women in the gospels?

7. What encourages you from the examples of women in the early church?

8. Pray that God will give you the names of two or three other women who would meet with you to pray about developing a Women's Ministries program in your church.

2
Called to Ministry

Called to a Woman-to-Woman Ministry

*I*f we can see from Scripture that Christian women in general are qualified for ministry, is there a specific biblical ministry to which women are called? And, if so, are there any criteria that further show what kind of women are called to that ministry?

Let's look at a definitive passage, Titus 2:1-7, where Paul instructs the young pastor Titus in various aspects of his pastoral work.

> **You must teach what is in accord with sound doctrine. Teach the older men to be temperate, worthy of respect, self-controlled, and sound in faith, in love and in endurance. Likewise, teach the older women to be reverent in the way they live, not to be slanderers or addicted to much wine, but to teach what is good. Then they can train the younger women to love their husbands and children, to be self-controlled and pure, to be busy at home, to be kind, and to be subject to their own husbands, so that no one will malign the word of God. Similarly, encourage the young men to be self-controlled. In everything set them an example by doing what is good.**

Paul the apostle was writing to a young pastor, Titus, whom he had left on the island of Crete. Paul had evangelized and started small churches on Crete, and he left Titus with the responsibility of firmly establishing those young churches so that they would continue to grow.

However there were serious problems in Crete that were typical of any pagan society the gospel has penetrated. First, there were no role models to demonstrate what godly people were like. "In New Testament times, life in Crete had sunk to a deplorable moral level. The dishonesty, gluttony, and laziness of its people were proverbial."[1] There was no one to demonstrate what a godly husband and father was like, or to model how a Christian woman, wife, or mother was to act.

Second, we find in Titus 1:10 that false teaching was deceiving and confusing people to the extent that Paul says in verse 16, "They claim to know God, but by their actions they deny him." We have this same problem today. There are more evangelical Christians

---

1. *NIV Study Bible* (Grand Rapids: Zondervan, 1973), Introduction to Titus; notes at 1:2; 1:12.

in America now than ever before, and yet we are having less impact on society. Christianity is losing its influence and its power because it has lost its distinctiveness. Sometimes it is hard to tell the difference between believers and unbelievers. Therefore, we have a need for proper role modeling, just as did the people in Crete.

Many young women today come to Christ who have not been reared in godly homes. They may have had parents who were nominally Christian or attended church, but who at the same time did not demonstrate the life of Christ in their daily routines. These young women don't know what a godly woman, wife, or mother is like, and they need to have that modeled before them. And no one can model a godly Christian woman, except who? A godly Christian woman!

Third, like Crete, we have false teaching, and plenty of it. Without a biblical perspective, many women are confused, deceived, and dissatisfied. There is a biblical remedy. Titus 2 gives us the antidote for false teaching and wrong behavior.

The first element of the remedy is sound teaching. In Titus 2:1, Paul instructs Titus to "teach what is in accord with sound doctrine." In the Greek, the word *sound* means "healthy." In other words, the false teachings so rampant were sick and diseased. Paul starts with teaching. So often we try to change conduct without first appealing to the mind and will. But God always starts with right teaching. However, right teaching is only one side of the coin.

The second element of the remedy is for godly people to model correct behavior. There is a need for role models that reflect the life of Jesus Christ. Christians must be distinguishable from unbelievers. Christian women must know what living out the life of Christ looks like in the flesh. God through Paul instructs Titus himself to teach the older men, the younger men, and the older women, as well as to set for them an excellent example. But when the Lord speaks of the teaching and training of the younger women, His instructions to Titus change. Titus is to prepare the older women to teach and model for the younger women a godly lifestyle.

Why Have a Woman-to-Woman Ministry?

In a day of increasing moral failure among the pastorate, the wisdom of woman-to-woman ministry is obvious. Surveys indicate that as many as 90 percent of moral failures in the pastorate begin in counseling women. Women, by contrast, have the freedom to follow up other women to encourage them in personal matters. If women are allowed to do the job they have been called to do, temptation to immorality can be averted in the pastor's study.

However, there are numerous other reasons women are effective in ministry to women. Who but another woman can fully understand all the differing aspects of pregnancy and childbearing, postpartum blues, and PMS? Women understand the cabin fever that often attacks in the preschool years that I call "a season of little feet." Another woman understands the weariness and isolation that can result from chasing energetic little ones who communicate primarily in one-syllable words and liberally spread peanut butter and jelly on floors and walls. Another woman can lift the spirits of a disappointed young wife who is discovering that her knight in shining armor leaves rust spots in the bathroom and socks on the floor. The older woman can help the young wife laugh at her circumstances and can dispel the idea that any knight comes rustproof in a fallen world. An older woman can encourage her to love and have patience in her marriage. Another woman can share her own life experience in learning how to balance the differing and demanding aspects of managing a home, loving a man, and rearing growing children.

A wise older woman is also a resource in the case of sexual harassment or even abuse. She is available to listen, believe in, and intercede on behalf of a young woman trapped in a dangerous or abusive situation. She can assist her in finding help and support from the leadership of the church.

A godly older woman will point the younger woman to the only One who will never disappoint her and who is completely trustworthy in any and all of life's situations. She will instruct her from the Bible and from her own life experience in coming to know Him better.

What Is the Older Woman to Model for the Younger Women?

Jesus pinpointed loving God and loving others as the core truth of life. Therefore, we might expect that the lives of older women He desires to use to train younger women will reflect His priorities. Titus 2:1-7 (quoted earlier) describes the older woman God is calling to minister to younger women. It gives us an idea of the kind of woman God would like every younger woman to emulate. A study of the qualities these older women demonstrate will reveal the kind of relationship they have with God and how they handle significant relationships with others.

"Reverent in the way they live, not to be slanderers or addicted to much wine, but to teach what is good."

The first phrase, "reverent in the way they live," summarizes the kind of *positive relationship with God* the older woman is to demonstrate and how she will spend her time. The word translated "reverent" as used in the Greek language described a pagan priestess serving in the temple of her god. It carried the connotation of a full-time service of worship. Grasping that definition of "reverent" will help us to correct the misconception that life is compartmentalized into the sacred and secular. Rather, we will understand that God desires women who view *all* of life as sacred and see themselves serving God just as truly when they are teaching a Sunday school class or preparing well-balanced nutritious meals for an active family. A woman like this will pursue her personal relationship with God with a deep passion. She will value all of life equally, from the car pool to the corporation. She will understand that God desires to be part of our every activity, and that He needs women representing Him in all walks of life. Her personal commitment to Christ is an obvious qualification.

The second phrase, "not to be slanderers," says that *relationships should not be built on gossip and slander.* Those are superficial relationships that counterfeit intimacy but do not lead to love of others or to a greater love and dependence upon God. Indeed, such relationships divert the heart from a passionate pursuit of God and divide individuals from one another. Paul warned of these superficial relationships when he spoke of the danger for young widows who "get into the habit of being idle and going about from house to house. And not only do they become idlers, but also gossips and busybodies, saying things they ought not to" (1 Timothy 5:13-15). That is why the ability to keep confidences is imperative if an older woman is to minister effectively to a younger woman. As younger women share confidences, seeking God's perspective on the problems they encounter, much information is communicated that would be very damaging if repeated and much that may be shocking. It is important that the woman who is counseling a younger woman be nonshockable. The younger woman needs to feel loved and accepted as she communicates what is on her heart. That does not mean that the one who listens has to compromise and accept the young woman's sins. That is why an older woman needs a close relationship with God and a good knowledge of what God's Word teaches about moral living. But these younger women do need wise love and support if they are to choose to turn from sinful choices and move toward God.

This idea of trustworthiness is also a *protection for relationships.* The word *slanderer* is taken from the root word *diabolus,* or devil. Satan for centuries has used broken confidences, especially among women, to divide believers. A woman who is rooted in a deep relationship with God will not have the overwhelming need to pass on juicy tidbits to enhance her own popularity, and consequently her personal relationships will be protected.

The third descriptive phrase, "or addicted to much wine," adds another insight about the godly older woman. The specific Greek terms mean to be a drunkard. This phrase indicates how *not* to cope with life and the challenges of daily living. God *does not want us to avoid life and relationships by escaping* from them through drink. Escaping reality deadens the heart rather than developing character. I think that we could broaden the concept of addictive behaviors to include any kind of chemical dependence, as well as other escape behaviors, such as soap operas, shopping, or extreme busyness. If we have not learned how to face life, depending on the Lord and His strength, rather than running from it, we will have little constructive counsel to share with another woman.

I have a young friend who was addicted to romance novels. She loved to read and spent hours each week reading fictional accounts of beautiful, romantic love affairs in which the heroine was rescued from the mundane of daily life by the handsome and often wealthy hero who carried her off to "happily ever after." Susan began to notice that she was comparing her faithful and hardworking (if somewhat unromantic) husband most unfavorably to these fictitious heros. After discussing this growing addiction and praying with an older woman, she chose to put aside a seemingly harmless pastime and instead invest time in the study of the Scriptures. Her reading turned to biographies of men and women of God through the centuries. Her marriage improved.

If women are *not to settle for superficial relationships or avoid relationships through escape or addiction,* what is the positive instruction from the Scriptures? I believe that we find it in the phrase "Teach what is good." This command suggests that in addition to a passionate pursuit of God, an older woman will *invest her life in quality relationships,* especially with younger women, transmitting to the next generation what she has learned from God. By the time a woman begins to reach mid-life, her own family responsibilities are changing. Her children may be away at school or married. She will have more time to invest in the lives of younger women. Interestingly, younger women will often listen to an older woman in this relationship when they would not even listen to their own mothers. And mid-life women find younger women eager to learn from them, even when their own daughters might not.

The word translated "good" means morally good, noble, or attractive. That assumes that the teacher understands what is good. I believe that understanding what is good requires a working knowledge of God's Word. It is important not only to know what the Bible says specifically, but how to understand what it says in principle. Many of life's problems are not addressed verbatim in the Bible, but there are clear biblical principles that speak to current decisions. An older woman who has grown to know God and the Bible can share those principles with a younger woman as no one else can.

What Good Things Do We Teach?

The subject matter to be taught by the older women to the younger women is described in Titus 2:4-5 (*Amplified Bible*):

> **"Train the young women to be sane and sober-minded—temperate, disciplined—and to love their husbands and children; to be self-controlled, chaste, homemakers, good natured (kindhearted), adapting and subordinating themselves to their husbands, that the word of God may not be exposed to reproach—blasphemed or discredited."**

Reality and Integrity

To begin with, it is important to teach the younger women to take life seriously and honestly, to be "sane and sober minded—temperate, disciplined." Our counsel to them should promote integrity and reality. Those qualities make a significant difference in how a person lives. Escaping reality does not promote biblical living. Calling a younger woman back to "sanity" may involve recounting our own youthful "insanity" and how God brought us through similar experiences. That will require a willingness in us to be open and vulnerable. Although we should be able to share selectively and discreetly, the women we are counseling need to understand that their struggles are not unique to their marriage and children.

I remember a young woman who came to me after only six months of marriage. She spilled out tearfully to me her disillusionment with her husband and her fear that she had made a terrible mistake in marrying him. She wondered if it was too late to consider annulment. After listening briefly to the specific incidents they had experienced, I smiled gently and shared that what she was experiencing was common to almost every married couple in the process of learning to live together. My counsel to her was to go home, keep communicating, loving, adjusting, and forgiving—and to trust me that these adjustments could be made. I prayed with her and gave her a hug. About a year later she came to me all smiles and shared how much "things" had improved and thanked me for sending her back to the Lord and to her husband to perservere in the process of learning to share and give.

In the area of discipline and self-control, it is important that we understand that exhibiting those qualities does not just mean abstaining from impulses. (The inability to delay gratification is indicative of immaturity, and a growing ability to postpone gratification an indication of growing maturity.) It also means learning to yield control to the Holy Spirit. Doing that will involve not only study of biblical teaching but also modeling the importance of depending upon God in daily situations and choosing to yield to His control.

Praying together is an effective means of modeling how to turn a problem over to God. Many times I have stirred supper on the stove with one hand while holding the phone in the other and saying, "Let's pray right now and ask God for His wisdom." Over and over I have heard how God answered our prayers and how much the young wives were encouraged by our conversation. It didn't take time from my responsibilities, but it accomplished something of eternal value. It also demonstrated that God is available anytime as well as my own dependence upon His wisdom. A willingness to talk or to give a little word of counsel can turn a young woman to God and transform her whole attitude.

In addition to promoting integrity and reality, our teaching of young women should *focus on her primary relationships.* For a married woman that would be her husband and children. For a single, younger woman that might be her parents, siblings, or her roommate or business associates.

Love for Her Husband

We are clearly told that we should teach the younger women to love their husbands. The word used here is the Greek word *phileo. Phileo* is the love of human emotion, friendship, and enjoyment. I think that young women, especially newlyweds, need older women to teach them to be adaptable and patient, to enjoy their mates without demanding perfection. Many of us have learned this the hard way, but everyone doesn't have to learn everything by experience. I am amazed at how much help it is to simply explain to a young woman the basic differences between men and women. When they say, "He won't do this, and he won't do that," I say, "You know, that is very typical of most men."

They are often shocked and say, "It is? You mean it isn't just my husband not being interested in what I say?"

I recently had the opportunity of speaking with a couple who had been married for several years. As we discussed their difficulties, it was apparent that a common difference in the communication styles of men and women was a large part of the problem. When Leah inquired about what happened during Matthew's day at the office, he often replied, "Nothing." Conversation ended. Leah felt shut out and unimportant. As I was able to explain to Matthew that Leah was truly interested in the minor details of his daily experience, he was more than willing to give her more than just his usual bottom-line response, "Nothing." As we discussed the general tendency of men to condense and women to amplify, I could see the understanding brighten their faces.

As we talked further, it became apparent that Matthew often was frustrated at the lengthy accounts Leah gave him of her day with the children. She was willing to attempt to condense her stories to leave time for his. I encouraged her to develop friendships with other women who would enjoy hearing all the details.

There are other differences in the masculine and feminine viewpoints. Larry Crabb states, "Men are designed to enter their worlds of people and responsibilities with the confident and unthreatened strength of an advocate. Women are designed to invite other people into a non-manipulative attachment that encourages the enjoyment of intimate relationship."[2] Because our fallen natures hinder our being all we were designed to be, there will be differences. When those differences lead to conflict, a confidential talk with an older woman can allow feelings to be shared and attitudes to be adjusted.

Love for Her Children

Second, we must teach our younger women to love their children. We live in difficult days for children. With the growing abortion problem, many never make it to birth. Those who survive may experience all kinds of abuse from neglect to molestation. Often that has been the personal experience of our young friends. They do not know what a normal childhood is. Many are victims of incest and pornography. We must encourage these young mothers, as much as is possible, to choose to stay home and take care of their children during their younger years. I am aware that today many single mothers must work to support their families, and that's a difficult and different problem. It is another reason for having an effective Women's Ministries program so that the church can minister to the unique needs of these single moms. But even with those who must work outside the home, we can encourage them to look for child care in home settings where the child's experience is as close to a family atmosphere as possible, as contrasted to a structured day-care center. The statistics on the traumatic emotional effect on children whose primary care has been in day-care centers are frightening. Young women need older women to give the perspective and guidance during these years. (See Appendix 1, "Hard Truths About Day Care.")

Teenagers can be greatly assisted by friendship and counsel from a wise, older woman whose own children have passed through those turbulent years. In recent days Fern Nichols[3] has helped promote the development of prayer groups for school children called "Moms in Touch." A group of concerned moms get together to pray in response to the growing needs of children in school. Such groups provide an opportunity for mothers to pray for the specific needs of schoolchildren in a particular area.

Management of Her Home

I believe that this additional instruction, which reads in the *Amplified* version, "to be . . . homemakers, good natured (kindhearted), and adapting and subordinating themselves to their own husbands," also relates to the impact a wife's behavior has on her husband.

The area of home management is often neglected by the church because it is not considered to be spiritual, but secular. However, such a compartmentalization of life is not biblical. All of life is sacred. Therefore, it is important for the church to see home management as an appropriate subject of training of the younger women.

Since God assigns home management as the woman's area of responsibility, that

---

2. Larry Crabb, *Men and Women* (Grand Rapids: Zondervan, 1991), p. 212.
3. Moms in Touch International, Box 1120, Poway, CA 92074.

responsibility requires appropriate authority. First Timothy 5:14 says that women are to "manage their homes." The word *manage* literally means "to be house despot," or total ruler. Some, unfortunately, teach biblical submission in such a restrictive way that the woman's responsibility remains, but the needed authority to accomplish it is removed. Instead of being, as I believe the Scripture teaches she should be, the queen of her home, a wife often feels that she is just a hired servant. Perhaps it is in rejecting this inaccurate and undervalued role that many middle class women have abandoned the arena of the home, leaving it increasingly cold and empty, while they seek self-fulfillment elsewhere. There is no doubt that today the home and family have been severely damaged. Conversely, a home well managed by a loving woman who is given both appropriate authority and responsibility will give her the legitimate satisfaction of a job well done.

However, it is important to remember that neither marriage nor motherhood nor a career is intended to provide our deepest fulfillment or worth. Only Jesus Christ can do that. This is what we must teach women. However, many basic homemaking skills, necessary if one is to obey God's directions about home management, are greatly needed by young wives today. Many have come from homes where mothers didn't teach or model how to manage a home, or where mothers lacked the appropriate authority to manage with godly creativity. That means that there is a great need for the skills many older women exercise almost automatically—skills as in meal planning, cooking, baking, sewing, housekeeping, and time management. Those skills make the older women a valuable resource to young women today.

Does this aspect of home management relate to loving your husband? I believe that when a man returns home from a difficult day in the office (wrestling in figurative terms with the thorns and thistles of the curse of Genesis 3:17-19) and comes into a home that is orderly and welcoming, he will be deeply encouraged that his efforts are accomplishing something, somewhere. His home, at least, reflects some sense of order in a world of chaos. Here, in the orderly home, we, as wives, can reflect to him God's design of a loving environment. Here, when a wife responds with care and attention to her home and learns to adapt herself to her husband, she ministers to his deepest longings for respect and adequacy.

"Men are different from women. They feel meaningfully encouraged not by a strong advocate who moves toward them but rather by a woman who appreciatively and respectfully accepts their efforts to handle the responsibilities of life."[4]

A wife who chooses to take that supportive role in the marriage, adapting herself to her own husband, cooperates with God in demonstrating to her husband his unique value without in any way diminishing her own value and worth. Likewise, the wife who neglects the home and refuses to adapt to her own husband communicates to him a lack of appreciation for his contribution to the home and a disrespect of his worth and value. When home management is seen as a significant ministry to one's husband, the most mundane of tasks can take on eternal worth. Could it be possible that there might even be crowns for clean bathrooms, balanced meals, and all that laundry? I think so.

4. Crabb, *Men and Women*, p. 167.

Submission to Her Own Husband

Likewise, when a wife chooses to submit to her own husband, as to the Lord, she reinforces his value and worth as seen by God. She fuels his sense of being adequate for the task he is undertaking, even though he may be meeting resistance on the outside.

Unfortunately, the subject of submission has suffered distortion in the way it has often been taught. Such unbalanced teaching often causes women to grit their teeth at the mere mention of the word. Many women resent it, and more than a few men exploit it. However, it is important for men and women to understand that this is voluntary submission to a husband's leadership. It comes from a spirit of obedience to Jesus Christ. It is not something the husband is given permission to force upon an unwilling wife. The word used for the obedience commanded of children and slaves is a different word from the word for "submit." Submitting is our responsibility before the Lord. It does not mean that all women are to submit to all men, nor does it insinuate that women are inferior as persons to men. Jesus Christ chose to submit Himself in His humanity to the Father. His submission in function in no way diminished His deity. Neither does a wife who submits to her husband in any way diminish her personhood, but rather she demonstrates her commitment to and trust in God and ministers to her husband in respect.

Ephesians 5 instructs the husband to lovingly, sacrificially lead his wife and the wife to voluntarily submit to her husband's leadership. But neither can do those tasks without the control of the Holy Spirit. I like to picture biblical headship and submission not as a prison where a wife is restricted and oppressed, but as a greenhouse, where, under her husband's protection, provision, and with his blessing, she is encouraged to develop her full potential.

Kindheartedness, a Good Nature

As for the expression "kindhearted," or "goodnatured," Tim Hansel often asks the women in his audience a searching question: "Are you fun to live with?" A willingness to forgive and to adapt and to cultivate a sense of humor adds zest to any marriage. I have a friend who loves to clip out cartoons and humorous articles and put them on her husband's plate for a smile at the end of a difficult day. A smile goes a long way toward easing weariness and knitting relationships.

Purity

This characteristic is very significant as it is related to the subject of loving your husband. This teaching would include sexual chastity before marriage and fidelity in marriage. This biblical truth is desperately needed to counteract our present declining culture. Sex has been so distorted and defiled that many people are genuinely surprised at what the Bible has to say about it. Many people outside the church have been led to believe that Christians are prudish and against the enjoyment of physical intimacy. Nothing could be further from the truth. Every biblical prohibition against sex is of sex outside the marriage relationship. Within marriage it is to be fully enjoyed and celebrated. Indeed, an entire book of the Bible, the Song of Solomon, describes in vivid detail the joys of the marriage relationship. However, marriage was designed as a commitment without alternatives. In this day, when even Christians are engaging in immorality and divorcing in record numbers, we need to face this problem head-on with clear, biblical instruction.

Someone told me recently that her husband had deserted her and their four children because he was in love with another woman. He admitted that he knew what he had done was wrong, but that after the divorce and remarriage he would ask forgiveness of God and be restored. Does he think he's fooling God? However, I am afraid that his thinking is more prevalent than we would like to admit.

Sex within marriage is an important part of the ongoing relationship between husband and wife. Women need other women to encourage them to understand both the privilege and responsibility of the sexual relationship. A neglect of the physical aspects of marriage can put the relationship at risk. The Bible is clear that the physical relationship is to continue regularly except for a season of prayer for particular reasons (1 Corinthians 7:5). The decision for restraint must be by mutual consent and for a brief time. (And, of course, there are times when for reasons of health there must be abstinence.)

A woman committed to purity and faithfulness in the sexual area honors the Lord and is a blessing to her family.

Living So That the Word of God Will Not Be Discredited

Should there be need for further encouragement about the significance of woman-to-woman ministry, the verse concludes by pointing out that women who follow the examples of godly older women will provide no occasion for the Word of God to be discredited.

That statement underscores the fact that the world is observing the lives of those who claim to belong to God. When our lives look just the same as the prevailing culture regarding home and family, and when our character does not reflect purity and kindness—in other words, when we do not love our husbands and children in demonstrable ways—the world will discount the truth and validity of the Word of God.

A friend of mine once took the Dale Carnegie course "How to Win Friends and Influence People." At the end of the course the instructor challenged the class. "Men and women, I hope that you will use the material we have studied and that people will see our principles reflected in your lives. I can't think of a more disappointing experience for you than to tell someone you have taken the Dale Carnegie course and for them to reply, 'You? *You* have taken the Dale Carnegie course? I *never* would have guessed.'"

Several years later John encountered a mutual friend acquainted with his instructor. In conversation John told him that their mutual friend had been his instructor in the Dale Carnegie course several years earlier. To which, to John's amusement and amazement, the man replied, '*He, he taught* the Dale Carnegie course? I can't believe it! He is one of the most reclusive and unfriendly people I know!"

I have often reflected on this story as it contrasts what we *say* when we are talking about our Christian walk versus how we actually *live* our Christian lives. When the two don't match up, at least in measure, all validity is lost. Conversely, when our lives do reflect the truth of God, others will be drawn to God.

Jesus instructed us, "Let your light shine before men, that they may see your good deeds and praise your Father in heaven" (Matthew 5:16). First Timothy 5:10 says that a widow is to be "well known for her good deeds, such as bringing up children, showing hospitality, washing the feet of the saints, helping those in trouble and devoting herself to all kinds of good deeds." A woman's life well-lived in dependence upon God is one of the most effective tools for evangelism.

An effective Women's Ministries program can greatly enhance the development of this kind of lifestyle for women.

(For further exposition and practical application of Titus 2:3-5, see my book *The Influential Woman* [Waco, Tex.: Word, 1992]).

Questions for Study and Discussion

1. Read Titus 2:1-5. Why do you think Paul instructed Titus to train the older women but not the younger women?

2. Describe an older woman of your acquaintance who you think demonstrates a reverent lifestyle.

3. Why do you think slander and gossip might lead to superficial and destructive relationships? What activities might contribute to slander and gossip?

4. What addictive behaviors can be used as an escape from involvement for Christ in the lives of other women?

5. Discuss the concept of reality and integrity as related to the command in Titus to train the younger women to be sane and soberminded.

6. What do you think 1 Timothy 5:14 teaches about a woman's responsibility for her home? What are the practical outworkings of this responsibility regarding the handling of finances, the checkbook, time management, meal preparation, and home decorating, to name but a few tasks?

7. Which aspect of learning to love your husband was a new thought to you from this chapter?

8. How important do you think it is for the sexual relationship to be taught in a positive manner? What older woman in your church might you ask to teach on this subject?

PART 2
Consider the Field

You are God's field.
1 Corinthians 3:9

3
Identify the Needs

Several years ago the Women's Ministries program of Northwest Bible Church was in the place where you may be today. The newly elected Women's Ministries Board decided to take a hard look at the programs that had been used for many years. Much effective ministry had been accomplished through those programs, but the percentage of women participating from the entire church body was small, and many women, especially the younger women, were not involved at all. That prevented the intergenerational dynamic that is at the heart of God's plan for a Women's Ministries program.

This intergenerational need had become clear to me several years previously. I had been teaching women in retreats and Bible studies for a number of years. I was also teaching a weeky Bible study for women in a local church that had an outreach to women all over the area. The younger women repeatedly said how much they appreciated learning the Bible from an older woman who had been where they were. They appreciated relevant application of the Scripture to their specific concerns. My husband and I saw this as a specialized area of ministry and founded Titus 2:4 Ministries, Inc., in 1984, really to define what I was already doing. As I traveled to speak around the country, however, I found that this was a felt need among women everywhere. Then, in 1989, when my husband and I had participated in Lausanne II in Manila, we learned that this need for women to minister to women, for each generation to nurture and disciple the next, was being expressed by women all around the world.

At Northwest Bible the existing women's program was built around circles for Bible study meeting monthly in homes. Although there was the advantage of closer fellowship in these small groups, something seemed to be missing, and general interest was declining. After considerable prayer, the new board made the decision to suspend all activities for one year and invest that year in research and prayer. They began by developing and distributing the survey following this chapter to all the women of the church in order to determine their interests and needs.

In addition to surveying the women of the church, the women on the board contacted churches around the country that had successful and proved programs for ministry to women. They were looking for qualities these programs had in common that made them effective. The committee discovered several features common to these effective ministries.

- Women wanted more sessions, not less—weekly, rather than monthly
- Bible study, not projects or missions, should be the main focus
- Diversity was essential, for example, electives for interest
- Programs with a woman on the church staff had greater continuity and effectiveness

As we developed and refined these features, we identified twelve elements of an effective women's ministry. They are as listed below and will be discussed in the next chapter.

An effective Women's Ministries program will start with prayer.

An effective Women's Ministries program will know its people.

An effective Women's Ministries program will enlist church leadership.

An effective Women's Ministries program will have specific goals.

An effective Women's Ministries program will be led by women.

An effective Women's Ministries program will develop leadership.

An effective Women's Ministries program will be built on Bible study.

An effective Women's Ministries program will have variety.

An effective Women's Ministries program will provide support groups.

An effective Women's Ministries program will have an outreach.

An effective Women's Ministries program will encourage personal friendships.

An effective Women's Ministries program will be flexible and relevant.

Women's Ministries Survey

Now there are varieties of gifts, but the same Spirit. And there are varieties of ministries, but the same Lord. . . . But to each one is given the manifestation of the Spirit for the common good (1 Corinthians 12:4-5, 7).

What area of need would you like to see met by the Women's Ministries program?

_____	Worship	_____	Instruction
_____	Fellowship	_____	Evangelism

What are your areas of interest (check as many as you would like)?

_____	Community outreach	_____	Mothers' encouragement
_____	Hospital visitation	_____	Exercise
_____	Bible study	_____	Weight reduction support
_____	Discipleship	_____	International students
_____	Prayer	_____	Three Score or More
_____	Lay counseling	_____	Hospitality for new members
_____	Political action groups	_____	Missions
_____	Food ministry	_____	Church grounds beautification
_____	Sewing	_____	Support groups
_____	New skills (homemaking)	_____	Other _____

Age _____

_____ Were you active in a circle this past year? If not, why not?

_____ Do you work full-time outside the home?

Please use the space below and the reverse side for any comments or questions.

Questions for Study and Discussion

1. How large is your church?

2. When was your church established?

3. What kind of ministries to women have there been thus far?

   A. List the three most effective
      (1)

      (2)

      (3)

         (a) What percentage of your women attended?

         (b) What are the ages of those involved?

   B. List the three least effective
      (1)

      (2)

      (3)

         (a) What percentage of the women attend?

         (b) What are the ages of those involved?

4. What are the predominant ages in your congregation?

5. How would you describe your church—urban, rural, suburban? Other unique characteristics?

6. How do these characteristics affect your women or your planning for a Women's Ministries program?

7. List some of the ideas that have come to mind as you have read this material and prayed.

4
Develop a Philosophy

Toward the end of the last chapter we listed twelve elements of an effective Women's Ministries program. In this chapter we want to examine each of those elements in some detail, because we believe that a ministry to women that does not have a core philosophy behind it will flounder and ultimately fail.

An Effective Women's Ministries Program Will Start with Prayer

If you are the only one interested in developing a Women's Ministries program, begin to pray and ask God to give you one or two other women who would be willing to meet with you and pray. Include the pastor's wife if at all possible. As you three or four meet regularly to pray, begin to ask God about some of the following issues:

1. How open is the leadership of the church to a Women's Ministries program?
2. Do you presently have a program for women? How effective is it?
   a. Are you involved in the present ministry?
   b. How open are those involved to evaluation and expansion?
   c. Would the leadership meet with you to pray and plan?
   d. When should you involve your pastor as you begin?
3. What kind of resource people do you have among your church women?
4. Whom could you enlist for leadership and support for the ministry?
5. How should you approach both church leadership and other women?
6. What direction should your ministry to women take?
7. How would God have you begin?
8. How can God use you to encourage and strengthen your church?
9. How can God use you to encourage and strengthen your pastor?
10. Ask God to protect you from a critical spirit.

An Effective Women's Ministries Program Will Know Its People

Using a tool such as the survey given at the end of the previous chapter, develop an understanding of your particular group of women. Here you will acquire important information, such as how many women are working outside the home, the general age breakdown of your group, and how many still have young children at home. From this information you can begin to evaluate various specific aspects of a program. Should the group meet in the evening or in the daytime, or both? What has been the previous history of the Women's Ministries program at your church, and how will that impact your planning? How far do your women travel to the church? Is yours an urban church or a neighborhood church? The answers to each of these questions will influence the various decisions you make as you develop your program.

An Effective Women's Ministries Program Will Enlist Church Leadership

A key step in organizing a Women's Ministries program is to inform and educate the male leadership of the church, if they do not share the vision. It is a rare exception to find leadership that has a Women's Ministries program high on its agenda. Usually the leadership leaves that to the women to do for themselves, including paying the expenses. We can respectfully point out that there is nothing in the Bible about a youth, college, or singles' ministry, but there is a definite command for the older women to teach and train the generation following them.

Although we take an offering at our Women's Ministries programs, we are supported from the church budget for all of our expenses, including child care. This concept has developed as we have ministered over these past seven years. We continue to run a tight ship and do all we can to "pay our own way," knowing that if we are not completely successful we have the support of the entire church. (The offering is deposited in the general church fund.)

Some denominational churches have a women's organization already in place with a structure that has been the same for one hundred years: WMU, WOC, WMS. We are finding that these programs in their original form often do not adequately meet the needs of today's women without significant revision.

Organized and Thoughtful Planning

The women from Northwest Bible Church put together a written proposal (see Appendix 2 for an outline of what was contained in that proposal). They included quotations from well-known women about the need for a relevant ministry to women and quotations from women in their own church in response to the survey. They detailed the plans they had in mind. They demonstrated their conviction that a woman was needed on staff to administer the program. Then they invited the elders and their wives for dinner and presented each elder with a folder containing the program laid out clearly. They answered their questions and discussed the subject thoroughly. This thorough approach and the evidence the women offered convinced the elders, and, consequently, a salary for a minister to women was included in the next year's budget, and I was hired. Expenses for a Women's Ministries program were also budgeted—including child care expenses. I can't emphasize enough how important it is to provide child care at no cost to the mothers bringing their children. These women are the very ones we want to reach, and if we make the cost prohibitive we will defeat our own purposes.

A Protected and Supportive Environment

I believe the elders of Northwest Bible Church demonstrated the kind of enlightened leadership that is essential in order for a vital Women's Ministries program to thrive in a local church. It is imperative that the pastor and elders understand the need to provide for the women of the church. They have to recognize that women have needs only women can meet. And they must delegate that ministry to spiritually mature women who can design and implement the program. Church leadership for its part must provide the facilities, personnel, and money necessary as an integral part of the church program. Women should not have to run a bootleg program on the side that they support with bake sales and garage sales. I view the relationship of the Women's Ministries program to the overall church ministry much as the relationship of a wife to a husband. The husband provides the environment for the wife to accomplish the ministry given to her by God in the home. That supportive environment includes providing the finances necessary to accomplish their mutual goals.

An Effective Women's Ministries Program Will Have Specific Goals

The development of specific goals keeps a Women's Ministries program continually on track and provides a measure of its direction and effectiveness. Our goals were as follows:

- To minister to the needs of the church women to encourage their growth to spiritual maturity. This ministry will also include evangelism.
- To equip women to serve others in the church.
- To provide opportunities and encouragement for ministry to our community.

These are long-range goals that must be kept in mind as the whole ministry is planned and implemented.

An Effective Women's Ministries Program Will Be Led by Women

Of course, I am biased about the need for a woman on the church staff for women. Call her what you will—minister to women, associate pastor of Women's Ministries, director of Women's Ministries, or chairman (or coordinator) of Women's Ministries Board (or council). You may have to start with a volunteer, but don't give up the idea that this position is worthy of a salary, whether the woman filling it is a part-time or full-time staff member.

A staff person has the time to focus her attention on the needs of women, both corporately and individually. She can plan and implement long-range programs that have continuity. Because she meets regularly with the church staff, she can speak for women, correlate her ministry with all other church activities, and add the relational insight that women bring to everything. In most churches over half of the constituency is women, and they are usually unrepresented on the church staff. In a number of delicate counseling situations, I feel that I have been able to share with our pastoral staff the issue from a woman's perspective. They have heartily thanked me for it. A staff member is also more regularly available for personal counseling, which can become an important aspect of the ministry. Her being able to counsel women will provide the protective aspect of ministry mentioned earlier.

Here is an excerpt of a letter I received from a young woman that illustrates the importance of having the women's ministry directed by a staff woman:

> Your stability in serving at Northwest to the women is an intangible ministry. Your commitment through the years is an unspoken anchor in this society of constant change. The fact that you've been there, involved in women's lives, is one of the threads that binds the newer folks to the ones who've been involved for years.
>
> I remember being amazed at how open our discussion group was from the very beginning, and I think the fact that you had built into the lives of so many of those women for such a long time allowed them the freedom to open up.

At the present time seminaries and Bible colleges are graduating women who have been highly trained and could fill these positions if churches realized the need for a minister to women.

The goal of the staff woman should be to get others to do the job, not to do it all herself. She is a pacesetter, not a prima donna. When you give a woman an opportunity to serve in a position for which she is gifted, you set her up for success, and she will want to keep serving. That takes honesty, humility, and discernment on the part of leadership.

In addition, and equally important, a Women's Ministries Board will be the heartbeat of an effective Women's Ministries program. The size of the board will depend on the size of your church. To get started, if your church does not have a staff person for women, the pastor can appoint a woman with spiritual maturity and organizational skills to serve as chairman (or director) of Women's Ministries. Then she should pray and seek out other women to work with her as a team, women who have a love and vision for women. As your program develops, you will find that various categories of activities demand supervision. That is why it is important to have a board of several members, each of whom has an area for which she is responsible. Authority goes with responsibility. The coordinator should be free to be creative and innovative within the guidelines set by the board. No member of the board is a loose cannon doing her own thing. The board should discuss each area and cooperate with the person in charge of it. That will provide accountability, yet let each woman use the unique gifts God has given her. This freedom with supervision is the secret of achieving the variety that makes a program successful. The chairman (or director) cannot be a dictator who must have everything done her way. That may be difficult for her if she is a strong leader. Yet it is especially important to be flexible if you want to attract young women. They will not fit into our old forms and our traditional way of doing things. We should not elevate forms to the status of the inerrancy of Scripture. Never say, "We've never done it like that before!" or, "It won't work!" Be open to new ideas. Make the program meet the needs of your women, rather than forcing the women into an obsolete mold.

Last year in planning for our Christmas luncheon, Susan, the board member responsible for special events, came up with the theme of a Mexican fiesta. I am not overly fond of that cuisine and wasn't particularly excited about the menu or all the details required to pull it off. However, remembering my commitment to allowing flexibility and freedom, I agreed with the plan, though without much enthusiasm. The end result was an outstanding luncheon that everyone enjoyed and appreciated. I could have squelched this delightful opportunity had I demanded that every aspect of the program be as I would individually prefer it. And I would have robbed Susan of the opportunity to minister to the entire body with her creative and artistic gifts. I was glad to admit I was wrong.

Our Women's Ministries Board meets monthly for business. We do not have any men at our meetings, either elders or staff. The job has been delegated to us. We are, however, accountable to the elder board and must follow their guidelines and report to them when requested, but they trust us to do the job. The Women's Ministries Board also meets for prayer just before the Women's Ministries program on Tuesdays and every other week after the Women's Ministries program. As a staff person, I report to the associate pastor on a bimonthly basis.

The job descriptions for our board are found in chapter 7. We update them each year. The myth that if you give women an inch they will take over the church is just that—a myth. If you give women significant ministry in the very area God has commanded for them, a ministry to the many, very real needs of women, they will be so busy and so fulfilled that the resentment and restlessness they often feel will have no fertile ground in which to flourish.

An Effective Women's Ministries Program Will Develop Leadership

The first consideration in developing leadership is an understanding of giftedness. It is important to match people to the tasks for which they are gifted. Because I believe that God provides gifted women to meet the needs of each congregation, it is helpful here to consider what the Bible teaches about spiritual gifts. Some women do not realize that they have been equipped from the time of salvation with special abilities from the Holy Spirit to strengthen their fellow believers (1 Corinthians 12:7).

Someone has defined a spiritual gift as a supernatural capacity freely and graciously given by the sovereign God at the time of a person's salvation, enabling him to minister to others for the purpose of accomplishing God's work.

Because an effective Women's Ministries program must be a team effort, we must try to help women identify their gifts. We need to find out what individual women like to do and what they do well. We need, also, to observe where a woman's service is not effective. We in leadership should do that for ourselves as well. It is no sin to recognize that we don't do everything equally well. Where I am weak, someone else is strong, and if we are working together, her strength makes up for my weakness and my strength supports her weakness.

There are several reasons you and your women should understand and exercise your spiritual gifts. When we in leadership are careful to fit women into jobs that suit their gifts, they will enjoy doing them, do them successfully, and be willing to take on new responsibilities as their confidence increases. Conversely, when you place a woman in an area where she is not gifted, she often finds the job so burdensome and unrewarding that she is reluctant to serve again.

It Will Give You an Indication of God's Will

When people know how God has gifted them for service, it will be helpful to them to determine where God wants them to serve. However, I also believe that many times a person has more than one gift, so do not limit service to just the gift most often used or most obvious at the moment.

It Will Help You Set Priorities

If you understand your gift, it will help you resist saying yes to every opportunity that comes to you. You can choose to serve in areas fitted to the gift that God has given you, and you won't feel that nagging guilt for saying no to other opportunities. In fact, as you recognize the way the gifts benefit the Body of Christ, you will see that to accept something that is not your assignment will rob someone else in the Body of the opportunity to exercise her gifts.

It Will Help You Accept Yourself

Often when considering service we make the mistake of comparing ourselves to others with different gifts, particularly the public gifts, and begin to feel inadequate. When a woman discovers her own gift and begins to serve in that capacity, she experiences the satisfaction of serving as God designed her. That experience develops in her a growing sense of satisfaction and fulfillment and self-acceptance.

It Will Identify Areas for Development

Additionally, when a woman discovers her spiritual gifts, she then has direction for prayer and development.

For instance, if you have the gift of teaching, perhaps you would like to pursue further education or take seminars to develop your speaking and teaching skills. Perhaps you have the gift of exhortation or mercy. Maybe counseling training would sharpen and develop those gifts. If your gift happens to be the gift of giving, perhaps you would find a key place in the missions program of your church, studying the various agencies requesting support.

Gifts Mentioned in the New Testament

1 Corinthians 12

Message of wisdom	Message of knowledge
Faith	Gifts of healing
Miraculous power	Prophecy
Distinguishing between spirits	Speaking unlearned languages
Apostles	Teaching
Helpers	Administration

Romans 12:1-8
Serving
Encouraging
Contributing to needs
Exercising leadership
Showing Mercy

Ephesians 4
Evangelist
Pastor/teacher

The important thing to remember is that spiritual gifts are given not for our own benefit but for the building up of others in the Body of Christ. Therefore, we really don't have an option about using them. When a member of your physical body stops functioning the whole body is sick. The same is true when a member of Christ's Body does not use her gifts for the good of the rest of the members. The whole local Body suffers loss. Romans 12:5 tells us that we belong to one another. We are not our own to live life totally independent of one another, focused on pleasing ourselves.

I am all for pampering women and making them feel special, as they are, but we must also remind each one that she is uniquely gifted by God with influence in her sphere of relationships. We must remind each woman that she is responsible to God to use her influence to serve Christ by ministering to others.

If the gifts are so important, how do we go about discerning them?

How to Discern Your Gift

1. Start with prayer, individually and with others. Ask God to reveal your gift.

2. Study what the Bible has to say about spiritual gifts.

3. Ask God's people what they observe about your abilities and effectiveness.

4. Examine your strongest desires or interests.

5. Look for an opportunity to serve in that capacity.

6. Allow God to confirm by experience and the feedback of others.

7. Notice the area in which you experience joy and ease in exercising your gift with results beyond expectations.

Additionally, there are spiritual gift tests that help confirm or inform people about their gifts. One test is published by Church Growth Institute, P.O. Box 4404, Lynchburg, VA 24502. Trenton Spiritual Gifts Analysis (published by the Charles E. Fuller Institute of Evangelism and Church Growth, P.O. Box 91990, Pasadena, California 91109-1990) is another such test. We offered these tests to our women when I taught 1 Corinthians 12. Many women said that they were surprised at what the tests indicated, but they could see possibilities they had not thought of before. However, the tests should be confirmation of the other factors mentioned above.

I am often asked how we select members for the Women's Ministries Board. We do not have elections. Women are invited to serve. Since each member is committed to a two-year term, we stagger their terms so that only half go off the board each May. We start as early as January to discuss potential candidates for these positions. However, we are always looking for women to develop as leaders who have shown commitment to the Women's Ministries program. Here are some of our considerations.

> Women who attend regularly,
> who may have taught electives,
> who often volunteer to serve,
> who demonstrate responsibility and skill in service they have done,
> whose lives evidence a love for God,
> who love and care for other women,
> who are members of the church.

We also look at their giftedness. For instance, when we look for an outreach coordinator, we want someone who can organize, delegate, and supervise the various ministries under her care. When we want a hospitality coordinator, we look for a woman who is warm, creative, and hospitable in her own home. When the board agrees unanimously to invite a woman to fill a position, I call or visit personally with her.

After commenting to her about how delighted we are with her interest and enthusiastic support of Women's Ministries, I ask her several questions, such as those below, and give appropriate explanations and encouragement.

Are you a member of the church? Are you willing to become a member of the church?

If she is not, everything else I will say is dependent upon her joining. (We do not require church membership for participation in the Women's Ministries program, but we do require it for a board position.)

How involved are you this coming year in other activities?

If she has many commitments, I ask if any are ending soon. If none are, I suggest waiting for another year. If some are ending, I continue and explain the position that is open, describing some of its responsibilities.

Does this position suit your interests and your gifts?

It is essential to ask this question, and it will free the woman from a sense of guilt if she is truly not suited to the position.

Are you willing to make a two-year commitment?

As mentioned before, a two-year commitment allows for staggered terms and the training of new people. When setting up a board initially, it will be necessary to start with half of the members serving for one year and half for two. From then on only one-half will complete their term each year, and that will provide continuity for the board.

When the woman expresses an interest, I make clear from the start that we are asking that the Women's Ministries program take priority over her other activities outside her home and family responsibilities during her service on the board.

If she is involved in a parachurch organization, I always encourage her, but suggest that serving in the Women's Ministries program is a way to get to know the women of her own church and minister to them. I am very grateful to Bible Study Fellowship and other Bible study groups that help equip women to serve. We are not in competition with them. We need to put the women they have helped to equip into positions of significant ministry in the local church. This past year we had five positions on the board to fill, and I only had to make seven phone calls. But even more significant is the fact that this is the seventh Women's Ministries Board I've served with, and we have never repeated any person. I am particularly pleased that we are not always using the same few people, and that variety has resulted in our developing new ways to accomplish our goals. We are always grooming new leadership at every age. Our present board consists of women in their twenties, thirties, forties, fifties, and sixties.

The present chairman and I select the new chairman. We choose her from the board members who are serving their second year. There is a new chairman each year. Each one I have served with has been different in style, but wonderfully efficient and indispensable to me. We consult frequently, and she takes care of communicating with the board and Women's Ministries about responsibilities, opportunities, and coming events; chairs the board meetings; and generally assists all of the board members as they need it.

My job description is included in chapter 7, because the chairman will have to assume many of those responsibilities if you do not have a woman on your church staff.

We attempt to have the new board members selected by the beginning of the spring session in March, so that they can work alongside the women they are replacing and get familiar with their roles.

In May we have an overnight retreat including the old and new board where we evaluate every aspect of the Women's Ministries program. We examine job descriptions and amend those to accurately reflect what the job has become. We discuss the whole next year's program, change some things, and plan new activities. Nothing is a sacred cow. We won't compromise on essentials, but we want to use variety in our approach. We do everything we can to direct, support, and encourage each woman in leadership.

The best way to develop leaders is to balance supervision with freedom. Each individual has a personal style and creativity that we encourage her to cultivate. We nurture that development with affirmation, praise, and constructive help. For instance, some people find it hard to delegate—usually this is the perfectionist. We have to remind those persons that the more women are involved in anything we do, the more committed they will be. We are committed to developing women, not just putting on a program. So the delegation of responsibilities is more important than perfection of performance!

Delegation develops people, not programs.

An Effective Women's Ministries Program Will Be Built on Bible Study

The Bible should be the central focus of a vital Women's Ministries program. God's Word is what people hunger and thirst for, often without realizing that the Bible is what they need. You can get women to come to varied programs that interest them, but you will not have the steady spiritual growth desired without consistent teaching of the Scriptures as relevant to the lives of women today. The goal of an effective ministry should always be to develop maturity (Ephesians 4:11-13; 1 Peter 2:2).

However, a church program and Bible study cannot have the stringent rules some parachurch organizations have. Those rules suit their particular purpose and structure, but a church program must be designed to meet the needs of all the women of the church, and they will be at many different spiritual levels—young lambs and mature sheep. Since the Women's Ministries programs are also an opportunity for women to bring their neighbors and friends to a church-sponsored event, your audience will range from the unsaved and new believers, the scripturally untaught, to the spiritually mature and knowledgeable in the Scriptures.

That is why the main Bible teaching must include the gospel frequently for the unsaved, be clear for the new learner, yet also have depth for the mature Christian. That is not an easy assignment, but it is not impossible.

What and How Long to Study

Today's culture is not geared to lengthy commitments. We have found it advantageous to break the study year into three sessions of between six to ten weeks each. Our fall session begins in mid-September and ends in mid-November. That frees up the holiday season. The winter session begins the week after New Year's week and ends in mid-March. We take one week off during school spring break and hold the spring session from late March through mid-May. This approach makes it possible to study different subjects each session if we desire to.

There are many advantages to these shorter, complete sessions. For one thing, it is much easier to get a teacher for six, seven, eight, or nine weeks than to find someone willing to teach from September to May. That is true of securing elective leaders as well. I am often asked what material we use for Bible study. Our teachers have always prepared their own studies, but that is not a requirement. We have had studies of Bible books, character studies, and topical studies. Beginning with several short sessions can facilitate your start-up.

Some of the Bible series I have taught over the past several years are available on audiotape. Those are listed in Appendix 3. They can be ordered if they would be helpful to your group. Individual questions that allow a person to study the passage before they come to class will challenge the serious student and help the new one learn to use the Bible in personal study. Everyone won't answer the questions, but those who do say without exception that they benefit from them. Examples of questions for this home study are also in Appendix 3.

In addition, many excellent study books by women for women are available in bookstores. Some authors I might suggest would be Jill Briscoe, Cynthia Heald, and the authors of the various studies in the Women's Workshop Series.

Who Will Teach?

Who will teach? This is where much dependence on the Lord is necessary. First, the teacher should be a woman. I have surprised men when I have been invited to speak to them in seminary classes, and I've stated, "Women can teach and apply the Scriptures to women better than men can." When I humorously observe that most of their illustrations come from football, baseball, or the military, they usually get my point. A woman teacher has an empathy and understanding that communicates to women. Women will respond more openly to a woman and will come more readily for personal counsel, which is a vital aspect of ministry.

But suppose you think you don't have a woman in your church who can teach. Does that mean you must go outside your church for leaders? Not necessarily. I am persuaded that God gives each local body the spiritually gifted people necessary to bring that particular body to maturity, including spiritually gifted women, so I believe there probably *is* a woman in the church who can fill this role. Pray for guidance. I cannot overemphasize the importance of praying about every aspect of your program. Also, be very careful that you look for a person who teaches the *Bible*. It is easy to be captivated by a good storyteller or someone with a charismatic personality who just talks about emotions and experiences, or who keeps you laughing. She might throw in a Bible verse here or there, but that is not systematic Bible teaching, and you will not have steady spiritual growth from that type of message.

Is there a woman in your church who teaches a home Bible study? Is there a woman who has been involved in parachurch Bible studies, such as Bible Study Fellowship or Community Bible Studies? Is there a person who always blesses you when she teaches? Is there a woman all consider to be a godly example and knowledgeable in the Scriptures? Ask her if she would be willing to teach one lesson or a four- or six-week session in the Women's Ministries program. Start small. Maybe she has prepared a series for use elsewhere. You can evaluate her effectiveness in speaking to a large group. Some people are very effective in small groups, but not as much so in larger groups. We try to look for women who project a personal warmth and love for women—a woman with compassion and humor. The teacher is as important as a role model as she is as a teacher.

If you find that you truly do not have anyone in your church who can take on the task, you could begin by asking a good teacher in the community to start you off— but try not to depend on importing people. One of your primary goals is to develop the gifts of your own women, and that will never happen if they keep seeing "experts" do the job.

One church in our area asked me to start their Bible study series. I told them that I would come and teach a seven-week series at the end of their Women's Ministries year if they used their own women before that. They didn't think anyone would do it, but they found three women willing to take four weeks each. I came in at the end of that year and taught the seven-week series, but they have never needed me again because they had found several in their own body willing to develop their gift of teaching. Keep praying and expecting!

An Effective Women's Ministries Program Will Have Variety

Variety in the Weekly Program

We have found that dividing our weekly program into two segments has met a variety of needs. In the first part of the program we meet for Bible study all together. Then we allot about fifteen minutes for announcements, service opportunities, testimonies, special music, and an offering. During the second half of the program we offer various electives or interest groups. These range from developing spiritual and practical skills to support groups. An extensive list of electives we have offered in the small groups follows in chapter 7.

These small groups accomplish several things. First, they enable women to get to know each other because the group is smaller and they meet for several weeks. Many friendships start here that continue.

Second, the women learn some skill (spiritual or practical) that they have needed or wanted to learn. So they grow in ability and confidence.

Third, the women learn to care and pray for each other, because fifteen minutes of the elective time is allotted for sharing and prayer. Many women pray aloud for the first time here in this small group, because it's safe.

Fourth, leading these groups provides many women an opportunity to serve the Lord with all of their skills. They are not limited to only teaching the Bible or working in the kitchen or nursery. If, as Scripture teaches, all of life is ministry, then the professionals—the lawyer, financial planner, nurse, and counselor—can profitably share their knowledge with us and increase their impact and ministry. The homemaker can teach basic skills, such as cooking, sewing, time management, and hospitality. The mature mothers can teach child-rearing from babies to adult children. All of life's training and experience are resources for the electives. This greatly expands opportunity for ministry and leadership development.

Fifth, the electives are an obvious way to spot new leaders for Women's Ministries. Most of the women on our board have helped teach an elective. Many continue to do so after their term on the board is over.

	Program Schedule
9:15-9:30	Coffee and fellowship
9:30-9:40	Group singing
9:40-10:30	Bible lesson
10:30-10:45	Announcements
	Recruiting, offering, special music
10:45-12:00	Elective time
	(including 15 minutes of prayer and sharing)

We hold an orientation for the small group leaders before the fall session of the women's ministries program to go over the elective leaders' guidelines and to provide some training on how to lead a small group. A resource book we suggest is *How to Lead Small Groups,* by Neal F. McBride (Colorado Springs: NavPress, n.d.). We tape the orientation session so that new leaders can listen to it and read the book before the winter and spring sessions, when it is difficult to hold another orientation session. In chapter 7 we have provided a copy of our handout of guidelines for elective leaders.

Special Events

Our women look forward to our annual retreat. This retreat has several purposes. One is to provide an opportunity for the women to nurture existing relationships and to build new ones through small and large group activities. A second and equally important purpose is to have a concentrated time of Bible teaching from a skilled Bible teacher. Third, in our world of pressure and demands, retreats provide an opportunity for reflection, restoration, and refreshment for our women.

Many of our women invite friends and family to the retreat, knowing that they will have the opportunity to understand the message of the gospel. We always inform our retreat speaker that we will have those who do not know Christ in our group.

In addition, the retreat provides for an intergenerational contact as well as an opportunity for our women who work outside the home to get better acquainted with those who do not.

Retreats take a great deal of careful planning and are the responsibility of the special events coordinator. She recruits committees and delegates to them the responsibilities of registration, skits, free time activities, and hospitality. The speakers are chosen by the board after we listen to tapes. A breakdown on planning and the committees needed is included in chapter 7.

During the summer we also have two or three "Saturday Specials," a one-day event complete in itself. These are held in June and July and include Bible teaching, or a missionary speaker or a book review, and three or four elective workshops. These "Summer Specials" provide an opportunity to keep in touch during the summer months and also expose new people to our Women's Ministries program.

A Christmas luncheon, a mother-daughter dinner, or similar day or evening special events provide other opportunities for inviting friends and family to visit our Women's Ministries program. A special speaker is invited by the board, and a theme is set to use for publicity and decorations. Sign-up sheets are used to enlist helpers for the decorating and for kitchen help. These service opportunities provide an entry point for new people to take small involvements and gain a sense of ownership of the ministry. Many of our board members began by helping out in these small ways. We are constantly on the lookout for interested and faithful people who are willing to serve others. Chapter 7 will include a checklist for planning a special luncheon.

We add variety by changing our format for the last week of each session in a number of ways. First, we specifically plan for the format to be a luncheon for the day group and a dinner for the evening group. (Suggestions for menus are found in chapter 7.)

Second, the program on the day of the luncheon is different, as well. We may or may not have the full Bible lesson. We sometimes have a speaker from one of our outreach ministries, e.g., Crisis Pregnancy Center, share its ministry. Or sometimes we have some of our own women report on the missions trips they have taken.

Third, we do not meet in the elective groups that day, but rather use that time for women to give testimonies about what the electives they have participated in have meant to them. Sometimes we set up tables to display the various things that were made during the electives.

Fourth, we have the teachers for the next session give a brief preview of their classes. We might have a question-and-answer time from the Bible teacher. This seems to be a favorite. Each week we have a box available for anonymous questions, and the question-and-answer session provides an opportunity to cover several of those.

We usually have some special music and generally a good time of fellowship. We have extended nursery these days, and ask the mothers to bring a sack lunch for their children.

The end-of-session luncheon (or dinner) has proved to be a good time to invite women who don't usually come to Women's Ministries, to whet their appetite. It is also a time to verbally express appreciation to each elective leader and to give each a small gift.

Your church facilities will affect your ability to do some of the things I have mentioned, but I have found women to be most creative in planning events and programs that provide warmth and fellowship under all circumstances.

Special Music

Music speaks to the heart. Special music provides an opportunity to prepare the women's minds and emotions to receive God's Word. It serves almost as an emotional glue, stimulating feelings of fellowship, love, reverence, joy, peace, adoration, humility, and awe. Beautiful poetry set to music often expresses our emotions in ways that would not be possible through words alone. It focuses our attention. Music is a wonderful way for many women to share their gifts and talents with the group.

An Effective Women's Ministries Program Will Provide Support Groups

Many women feel isolated today. Some are badly damaged from their background or in their present situations. We have to face the reality that what is going on in the world is going on in the church. Women you sit next to in church have been victims of incest and child abuse. Some have had abortions. Some have discovered that their husbands are homosexuals. Some have had husbands divorce them for another woman. Some are having affairs with other men. Some are struggling in very difficult marriages. We started our support group program with an elective using the spiritual twelve-step program one of our women was trained to use. Since then, that group has met regularly on another day. An elective called "Motherhood, Not a Job for Sissies" was held our first year, 1985. Those young mothers did not want to end that mutual support, and so Mom-to-Mom has been meeting monthly ever since at a different time from the regular program. They have programs that meet their needs. They have a prayer chain and service opportunities different from those offered in the larger Women's Ministries program.

One of our women conducts an abortion recovery course that helped her after eighteen years of dealing with the guilt of abortion. This course has been a blessing and source of healing for the women who have taken it. It goes without saying that this group is confidential and that members' names are not publicly known.

One day a woman suggested to me that women like herself who had mastectomies could support other women who faced that crisis. I was delighted with the idea. We met with several other women in the church who had experienced mastectomies, and they set up goals and guidelines. They named themselves "The Uplifters." They are immediately at the side of any woman who faces even a biopsy, and they continue to support those who actually have a mastectomy. One of the ways they serve everyone is to arrange each year for the mobile unit from Baylor Medical Center to come to the church campus for mammograms at a reduced rate. Out of this group a monthly support group, CanSupport, was formed for those who are suffering from any kind of cancer or who are caring for a cancer patient.

We have had electives in marriage enrichment and the ministry of encouragement that have continued to meet on their own afterwards. The Women's Ministries program is an umbrella under which all of these groups function. That gives them security, status, and accountability.

The ministry of the support groups often brings to the surface situations where there is a need for personal counseling. If a leader feels she is out of her depth, she refers that person to me. If I think it's beyond my range, I refer the woman to Christian counselors we trust. But we also have a lay counseling group, called "Care Givers," a core of wise, mature women, each of whom can take a troubled person under her wing and be a friend to her. We offer classes each year to increase their counseling skills. I often refer women to them and ask one of them to step in and help someone out. They are having a very effective ministry.

As you can see, the variety is an ever-developing aspect of the creative ability of women to respond to others and to our culture. Chapter 7 contains a detailed listing of many of these groups.

An Effective Women's Ministries Program Will Have an Outreach

A failure to reach out into our community would condemn our ministry to eventual self-destruction. Missions begins at home and extends around the world. We are committed to providing opportunities to serve in the church and in the community. This outreach has become an extensive part of our ministry and developed even more after our program was well established. It also provides a place where some of our older women who have been faithful and involved in missions outreach for years can plug into the overall Women's Ministries program.

We send tapes of our weekly Bible studies to all the missionaries our church supports. We take interest in special missions projects, personally and financially. We recently helped support some of our women who went to Romania and to the Soviet Union to minister. We help sponsor many of our young people for short-term missionary trips.

At our annual week-long missions conference, we have women missionaries at our regular Women's Ministries session. They give us insight into missions from a woman's point of view. For many of our women, the program is their first personal exposure to world missions.

In addition, our women have been involved in a multitude of local outreach programs since we began the Women's Ministries program. Each year new opportunities surface; one outreach may replace another as we grow, expand, and adapt. (In chapter 7 we have a list of the various kinds of outreach that have proved effective for us, as well as some suggestions to stimulate your own thinking.)

Here are excerpts from letters from some of our foreign missionaries demonstrating the effectiveness of Women's Ministries in other cultures.

My husband, children and I live in a small village that is 100 percent Muslim. At present we are learning the language and are in the early stages of Bible translation. The government does not know we are doing this, otherwise we would be asked to leave! Therefore, my husband has to hold a secular job, which has been teaching English, but now he has permission to do full-time "linguistic research." We have three small children: 3½-year-old twins, a boy and a girl, and a 1½-year-old girl.

With this background, I would like to tell you how much I enjoy the cassette tapes of your Bible teaching that NWB sends me. After listening to the series on Hebrews, I wondered, "Who is this who can speak directly to me on the other side of the world?" The highlight of my week is to put the kids down for a nap and listen to your tapes. What you say seems, often, to apply to me even though I'm in a foreign country living a different lifestyle from women in the U.S. What a blessing you must be to the women in Dallas. And what an encouragement you are to those of us with young children. At one point (or maybe several) of wondering why I am here in this strange culture with little children, not understanding the language or the customs (people), you reminded me that my feelings are normal and that this is a special time, not only for my children, but for me. It is also good to be reminded that as Christians we are all foreigners, even in our own country.

[From Europe] The main reason I am writing to you is to ask a favor! I used to teach Bible Study in English to internationals living in Milan. All of the ladies have since moved away, mostly to the States where they have found good churches. My closest friend from the study is married to an Italian, and they now live in a villa outside Florence. Her husband is very hostile to her faith, even to the point of continually throwing out her Bible if he finds her hiding places! This has gone on for years. It is hard for her to get to church on Sundays since there are none closer than thirty to forty minutes' drive.

So her main fellowship is a women's Bible study at an Anglican church near her town. She began to attend in the hope that she might provide some good biblical input. There are a couple of other strong believers in it, too. I had given her a series of your tapes, and she promptly took them to the study—and the girl leading it had never heard anything like them! So, basically, you are having a tape ministry in Italy. They keep asking for more tapes. They have just about cleaned me out of just about everything that the church has sent me for the last few years and are asking for more. Could you get someone to send me another set of the Hebrews series, "Winning God's Approval"? I'm sending them the sermon tapes as well from the church services, but they like the ones from a woman particularly!

After reading a letter one week from one of our missionaries who was experiencing a particularly difficult time, several of our women wrote to her and called with words of love and encouragement. This letter followed:

I guess many of those sisters who heard my letter prayed for me because I feel much stronger now. Sometimes I feel tempted to write only about the bright side of the ministry, but transparency brings encouragement and prayer from the body, like a stream of red blood cells.

An Effective Women's Ministries Program Will Encourage Personal Friendships

Women are longing for friendships with other women. James Dobson reminds us that the loneliness and isolation women feel today is not because men have changed in the last century. It is because there has been a breakdown in the communication between women and women. With the increased mobility people have and the breakdown of the extended family, women's opportunities for relationships have been greatly curtailed.

In previous generations women did things together—cooked, sewed, quilted, canned, raised children, and mostly talked! We have largely lost that sense of community and today the church must step in and help women get to know and love each other, filling the gap left by the disappearing extended family. Serving on committees and boards together, taking an elective together, going on retreats, praying together—all provide opportunities for friendships to develop. Fellowship is more than coffee and cake; it is working together toward a common goal.

Here at Northwest we also have developed a program of intergenerational friendships called Heart-to-Heart. This program has done much to promote honest, caring friendships among our women. Details about how to implement this program, along with forms needed, are included in chapter 7.

An Effective Women's Ministries Program Will Be Flexible and Relevant

A Women's Ministries program that is supported by church leadership provides a protective umbrella under which its activities can function. In that way there are not many independent and overlapping things going on with no central coordination or focus. There is accountability, which is essential. Of course, we did not start out with all of the programs just outlined. Many were suggested or added as we saw needs surface and as people were available to implement them. Just recently I met with a core group to organize an evening class for business women that will discuss the issues women face in the marketplace. The class has been requested by several women. Our approach has been first to find a leader, then to work with her in setting goals and guidelines. I told this group that we had only two basic requirements: (1) They were part of the Women's Ministries program and thus accountable to us, and (2) their lessons needed to be based on Scripture. With those basics in mind, they were free to do whatever would meet their needs.

Just last week another woman called and said that she would like to organize a support group for women who are caring for aged parents. I told her to pursue it, and we would help organize it. I think this group will be a great encouragement to women who are at that stage in life. We recently started a support group for widows. They call themselves Hand-in-Hand.

As you can see, the possibilities are limited only by the creativity and size of your group.

Summary

As you begin to pray and plan, assess your particular situation along the lines of the twelve characteristics of an effective Women's Ministries program. Use the questions following this chapter to begin to focus on your areas of strength and the areas where you need development.

Questions for Study and Discussion

1. Review the twelve elements of an effective Women's Ministries program.

    a. List the features that are presently part of your ministry for women. Based on this chapter, can you think of ways of improving them?

    b. List the areas of your ministry to women that need development. Can you think of women who could be effective leaders for these new programs?

2. Which of the elements of an effective Women's Ministries program seem particularly relevant to your situation, and why?

3. Where and when do you think you could begin?

4. List five specific ways to pray about your plans.

5
Consider the Culture

Now that you have begun looking at your individual situation and developing a philosophy especially suited to your women's ministries program, it is important to consider the culture in which you will be working.

Recognize the Differences in Age Groups

Kerby Anderson in his book on the baby boomer generation, *Future Tense* (forthcoming, Thomas Nelson), calls attention to aspects of our culture that will significantly affect your planning for a Women's Ministries program. Seventy-six million people were born in the United States between 1946 and 1964. At least half of those people were women. That means that there are nearly 38 million women between the ages of twenty-seven and forty-five. This is the first complete generation raised on television. It has also been influenced by the turmoil of the sixties, the period which launched the feminist movement. Although the feminist movement has produced some positive results, there are some negative ones as well.

Women today have been indoctrinated with the idea that their personal worth is to be found only in competing with men in the marketplace. Homemaking and mothering skills have been devalued, so that the woman who stays home and cares for her children often feels guilty for doing it and enjoying it and is questioned by those who don't.

Consequently, those necessary skills that many of us older women learned at our mother's side in previous generations have not been taught to the baby boomer generation.

Many young women have not been trained to manage a home, cook nutritious meals, live on a cash basis within their income, or do any of the things, such as sewing and knitting, that everyone almost automatically learned in earlier years.

The sixties were also a period of affluence, national optimism, and parental indulgence. This generation has the attitude of entitlement ("I have it coming to me"). It demands personal freedom, self-expression, and self-fulfillment as a constitutional right; it values variety and choice. Baby boomers have smaller families and more two-income families.

During the 1950s, in over 70 percent of the homes the husband was breadwinner and the wife was home with the children. In 1990 this pattern had been reversed to the point where only 30 percent of the families followed the traditional pattern. Sixty-eight percent of women with children under six are in the work force today. It is projected that by year 2000 that figure will be 90 percent.

In a lecture, Kerby Anderson described baby boomers as follows:

> Baby boomers are *fickle*. This is not a culture where loyalty is a virtue. If they don't "get something out of it," they just go somewhere else. *Commitment* to friends, marriage, church does not come easily for most. Baby boomers are *cynical* and distrust institutions, such as the "organized church." They are *secular*—much less involved with religion than their parents. They are *lonely*. 24 percent of adults live alone. But for those living with someone, psychologists have invented such terms as "crowded loneliness" and "living together loneliness" to describe this generation's need for fellowship and intimacy. They are easily *distracted*—TV, short attention span, fast pace, lack of discipline. Spectators, not participants.[1]

Consider the Unique Needs of Single and Career Women

There has also been an enormous growth in the number of singles living alone. In the 1950s only 6 percent of the population lived alone as compared to approximately 24 percent today. That figure includes, of course, those who have never married, the widowed, and the divorced. Single parent families are increasing every year. No one can even measure the damage that divorce is having on the children—and these children are the parents of our next generation.

How can we minister to singles? This is an increasing concern of the local church. One-third of my home church is single; therefore, we have a minister to singles and a strong singles' ministry. I recognize that most smaller churches do not. However, even with our active singles' ministry, we have found that single women still desire to be connected to women of the church. They get tired of being with just their peers. There is a lack of reality in a life where there is no connection to the generations before you or after you. Single women also have many questions, questions that need the counsel of older, spiritually mature women. Consider these questions I was asked to answer when I was invited to meet with a small group of Christian single women.

1. Can you offer encouragement for women who have not had the example of a Christ-centered marriage in their homes that their own marriages can be different, and how can women learn to recognize when their relationships are following the unhealthy patterns they learned as children?

2. Define submission and describe how we are to apply it in the following situations:
   a. with men at work
   b. with men friends
   c. in our church

---

1. Kerby Anderson, lecture notes taken by Vickie Kraft, 1991.

d. in dating relationships

e. with Christian versus non-Christian men

3. What are our natural instincts and desires as women? How can we constructively deal with those desires in our current position as single women? How can we be content?

4. How should we handle the situation when a single friend becomes pregnant?

5. When we are interested in a dating relationship, is there an appropriate way to pursue it?

6. If we have already given up our virginity, is there any way we can be pure again before God, and how can we deal with the guilt that may be involved?

7. What kind of ministry options are appropriate and available to single women?

Because we offer an evening program, many of our singles and career women have taught electives. They have also been involved in outreach and missions. They are generous in their giving to special projects, and they love the Heart-to-Heart relationships, both as Juniors and Seniors. (This program is described in detail in chapter 8.) The abilities that have made them successful in business can be tapped for use in the family of God. That's why I'm so thrilled to see some of them take the initiative to form an evening class for business and professional women.

We also have to recognize that the number of single parents, especially single mothers, is increasing. We in the church can do much to help, and we need to find creative ways to do that. For instance, our newly formed Men's Ministry recently had a work day where several groups of men went to the homes of single mothers and widows and did repairs and yard work. The Heart-to-Heart Friendships have helped here, as well.

Recognize the Emphasis Placed on Sexual Relationships Today

Two million couples live together today without marriage. Some of those couples come to church on Sunday and are a part of your congregation. This is a troublesome undercurrent that must be considered as you plan for your particular style of women's ministry. For instance, today the family is considered an economic, not a social, unit. Productivity is considered the measure of personal value. Children have low priority and adult self-fulfillment has highest priority. We are almost in an adult-oriented culture.

The Impact of the Culture on Your Congregation

These are the people the church must reach: the baby boomers themselves or the children of baby boomers. And we will only be able to reach them as we realize their characteristics and needs and provide ways of meeting them. Insisting on old methods will end in failure. How aware are you of the impact of this culture on your congregation?

On the other hand, we can't throw out good methods that have ministered effectively to the older generation. Somehow, we must try to incorporate something for everyone. In evangelism we should use every method that will reach the unsaved; in discipleship we must not compromise biblical standards and give in to what the world says we must do—but we can adapt our methods. The Women's Ministries program is really discipleship at many levels simultaneously.

Give Your Program an Umbrella of Protection and Accountability

That is why it is important to have a Women's Ministries program that can be an umbrella for the activities needed for young and old, new and mature believers. A Women's Ministries Board that is accountable to church leadership but has the authority to plan, promote, and implement programs is really the only practical way to go. It will relieve the pastor and male staff of a burden they are unable to carry.

Provide Child Care

Good child care is essential if you want to have a successful program. Child care is often seen as something the women have to provide for or do for themselves, but it is usually the mother of young children who can't afford to pay each week for several children, so she just won't come. And if women have to take turns volunteering in the nursery, they often drop out. Yet these are the very young women we are commanded to teach and train. Child care is a legitimate need, as much as are facilities and utilities. Get paid workers. Many women will welcome the extra money and will commit themselves for the year. Retired women on Social Security make wonderful workers. You may take an offering each session to help defray the costs. In that way everyone shares the burden, not just the young mothers. But ideally, the church would see this as its responsibility and provide for it in the overall budget. You can see that a lot of re-education may be involved.

Give Speakers a Tangible Sign of Appreciation

When you invite a woman to teach a Bible study or speak at a retreat or at any of your meetings, you should thank her in a tangible way. At Northwest we do not pay anyone who attends this church for whatever service they do here. That is their ministry to their own church family. However, we do show them our appreciation with a gift of some kind—flowers, a quality piece of china or crystal, or perhaps a framed verse in calligraphy. We also send a thank-you note as well as offer personal thank-yous.

But when we invite someone to come from another church or place to speak or teach, we pay their expenses and give them an honorarium—a check (1 Corinthians 9:11; Galatians 6:6). There is an archaic idea that a woman doesn't need to be paid since she is supported by her husband. There is no connection between the two. A laborer is worthy of her hire. When we consider the time invested in preparation before coming and the time taken from the speakers' own lives to travel and serve us, it would be most ungracious of us to not acknowledge their service tangibly. Money for the honorarium should be included in your yearly budget or added to the cost of the occasion, e.g., a luncheon ticket. If the speaker does not want to accept the money, that is her choice, but we should offer it. She should not be forced to contribute to our ministry. Let's not be stingy. God will supply the money if we give generously.

I was once invited to speak at a kickoff luncheon for a church some distance from my home. Besides my preparation time, the event took all of my Saturday morning and part of the afternoon. When I arrived, they pinned a little corsage on me and had a little book at my place. I appreciated them. What I didn't realize was that they were all they had planned to give the speaker. I waited for a couple of weeks, then called the director of their women's ministry.

I said, "Linda, this is a little awkward for me, but I wondered if you have a policy of not giving your speakers an honorarium?"

"We give them a little gift," she replied.

I continued, "A gift is appropriate if the speaker is from your own church. But when you invite someone from elsewhere, you should plan to cover their traveling expenses and their time and effort."

She was open to my suggestion, and about two weeks later I received a gracious letter thanking me for calling their attention to a grave oversight. There was also a satisfactory check included.

Securing Special Speakers

We often invite women from outside our fellowship to speak for special events, such as retreats. We want to be sensitive to their needs and appreciate the investment of their time as they come to share their gifts with us.

We begin by getting recommendations of effective speakers and trying to get an audiotape of something they have done previously. If possible, we secure this audiotape and listen to it before we even make a first contact. If that is not possible, we graciously request a tape of some message they have given.

In making this request, however, we try to avoid the kind of attitude demonstrated in the following excerpt from a letter I received regarding a speaking engagement:

> We are making a composite list of women speakers for future church retreats, etc. We would appreciate your sending a résumé of your ministry, listing any teaching, lecturing, or speaking engagements you may have done. An audiocassette of one of your speaking engagements, a copy of your theological doctrine, and specific details of fees charged would be helpful.

Try to remember that the person you are contacting is not applying for a position with your ministry. Rather, you are requesting her to come and share her ministry with you, so your first contact should be gracious, not demanding.

Generally our first contact is by phone. If we have listened to the tape, we are ready to see if that date of our retreat or seminar might be available on their calendar. If it is, we need to cover the points below in natural conversation. Here is an outline to follow to help you in securing special speakers.

1. Give the speaker a little background on your group, its age span, and how many participants you expect. Give her your name and phone number.

2. Discuss possible subjects, asking if she already has some retreat messages prepared. Ask her if she minds your taping the messages.

3. Determine if she charges a set fee, or if she would be able to work within your budget for speakers, which would cover all her expenses, including air fare, and would allow approximately $100 per message. It is important to realize that a retreat speaker is giving up from two to three days of personal time to be with your group—and you do not want to ask her to contribute involuntarily to your ministry. Find out if she prefers to make her own travel arrangements, or if she prefers for you to do so. You can call to remind her nearer to the retreat date to secure advance purchase tickets.

4. If you plan to have small groups, ask the speaker to send you either the discussion questions or the appropriate subjects for you to compile them.

5. Ask what special needs the speaker might have, such as lapel mikes or overhead projector. Ask her how you as a committee might be praying for her as you approach your time together. If the event is other than a retreat, ask what type of accommodations she prefers, i.e., a hotel or a private home. Be sure that the accommodations provide a comfortable atmosphere with privacy for study.

6. Give her an idea of the type of clothing needed—casual, dressy banquet, and so on.

7. Ask her if she is willing to counsel individually if there are those who desire it and time permits.

8. Confirm your conversation with a letter with the details you discussed.

The Event

1. Treat the speaker as you would a welcome guest in your home.

2. Assign someone to meet her and to sit with her and introduce her to others.

3. Provide a private room and bath at the retreat. Most conference centers have rooms especially for the speakers.

4. Provide a basket of fruit or flowers in her room to welcome her.

5. Thank her verbally from the front, giving opportunity for appreciation. Have the honorarium check ready to give her as she leaves.

Follow-up

1. A written thank-you is always appreciated, especially if it includes some comments and feedback.

2. Continue to pray for her ministry and the fruit of it in your group.

Special Problems

Majority Older or Younger

What about a church where there are mostly older women? How do you attract younger women? If you offer a program that has a Bible study that addresses relevant life issues and also offers electives that interest younger women, they will come if you invite them. This can be a wonderful outreach in your neighborhoods. We have women who come because a neighbor invited them or someone in a garden club invited them. They have come to know the Lord or grow in their faith as a result. When they experience the benefits of relationships with these older women, they will be committed to the Women's Ministries program and start to serve as well. The older women can be like a magnet attracting them.

But what if a church has mostly young women under forty? Then the pastor's wife, and the wives of the elders and deacons, may have to assume the older woman's roles. But you will need to personally recruit the older women that you do have. Make them feel needed. And remember, you can't do it all in one year. This is a process of ongoing development. We keep changing and improving our program each year, but we always keep our long-range goals in mind. We want to meet needs and develop maturity and leadership in our women and equip them to serve.

When Leadership Is Not Supportive

This is a very difficult problem. Sometimes the leadership is not supportive because the men sincerely believe that women should not have any positions of leadership at all. They take the passages that set limits on women (1 Corinthians 14:35 and 1 Timothy 2:11-14) and make them apply to every area of life, when they refer only to the public worship service. That is poor interpretation of Scripture. But it is hard to overcome, because it feeds a natural desire in many men to control. However, you will not get anywhere by being militant and demanding your rights. Gather a couple of other women and share your vision. Include the pastor's wife if you think she is open. Begin with prayer.

Then you might start by approaching your pastor on the basis of Titus 2, where the pastor is told to teach the older women so they can teach the younger. Ask him if he would teach a group of mature women who want to obey God's command. He might be willing to do this or provide for it to be done. It has been exciting to me to see women who have been sent to us by their pastors and churches to learn about a Women's Ministries program, with their expenses paid by the church.

In a church where you have a program that you need to change, you might do as our women did. Investigate, gather evidence, survey your own women. Plan a program that will meet your needs and suit your situation. Then approach your leadership. Speak to the pastor. Share your concern with an elder or deacon who may be sympathetic. Invite the elder or deacon board to dinner. Be organized and factual as you present your proposal. Trust the Lord to change minds and hearts.

But if you still have refusal, don't give up. Start a Bible study in someone's home and invite friends and neighbors. Have a craft day in another home. Ask God to give you creative ways to obey Him, and choose not to be a source of dissension in the church. He may give you men with changed minds, or He may change the men in leadership. Those are all possibilities. But we have seen that when leadership sees the blessings that a responsible Women's Ministries program brings to the whole church, they are supportive and enthusiastic. Frequently, elders have told me personally or written notes expressing appreciation for what the Women's Ministries program means to the church and to their own wives. Elders' and deacons' wives can be your biggest allies.

Let me add a word about the pastor's wife. Frequently, she is the one with the vision to start and lead a Women's Ministries program, and her interest is important, necessary, and effective. She should always be involved with the women of the church, and women love to have her participation. But as soon as someone else is capable of replacing her, it's a good idea for her to relinquish the leadership and continue to serve in another capacity. That way you avoid the criticism that the pastor and his wife run everything. The responsibility of leadership is to "equip others to serve," not to do it all ourselves.

Another possible situation is when you have a denominational women's program that most (or many) churches have. You can try to work within that structure and adapt it to some of the ideas we have given you in this workbook. You can suggest changes when you have your regional and national meetings. I have had the opportunity to speak at some of those conferences, and there is always interest in improving the denominational program. Methods should not be set in stone. If you can't introduce change without upsetting the applecart, then supplement the program with "Saturday Specials" or with a six-week Bible study or counseling course. Have a craft day. Take on a new outreach to the community. Start a clothes closet for the needy in your church and community. Form a support group for young mothers, or cancer sufferers. Branch out. You will always find someone with a special interest who will carry the ball for you. All of these ideas will allow relationships to flourish.

"Heart-to-Heart," our program of matching Juniors and Seniors described in chapter 8, is a good place to begin. It provides an opportunity for intergenerational relationships and can create the base needed for the full program of women's ministries.

Always keep your priorities in order. Bible study should be first and foremost because that produces spiritual growth and the motivation necessary to serve. Then variety to tap all the resources available to you and to equip women in all the areas where they have responsibilities. Encourage friendships, be available for counseling. Let God stretch you. No one is adequate in himself for this, but God is the one who makes us adequate and competent. He just wants your willing heart. He will work through you.

Now that we have looked at these considerations, it's time to dig in for yourself.

PART 3
Breaking Ground

When a farmer plows for planting, does he plow continually?
Does he keep on breaking up and harrowing the soil?

Isaiah 28:24

6
Develop a Design

We have already discussed the fact that women are qualified for ministry and called to ministry. You have begun to make an assessment of your present situation and have considered our present culture. Now you are ready to begin to develop a design suited to your particular circumstances and to draw together the various aspects of a Women's Ministries program and apply it to your own church.

I often hear the question, "But our church is not a big church like yours. How can we do what you do?" Just scale the program to fit your resources. You can have a smaller Women's Ministries Board—just big enough to cover your activities. You don't have to start with three sessions. Start with one in the fall and one in the spring. Have six-week sessions, or even less. Have a good, relevant Bible study, and then offer three or four electives, depending on their variety. Pair women up in teaching teams. Have an elective that is a potpourri of crafts, so that if a person is only good at one or two things, she will still be able to share these skills. We had a very successful elective on how to have family devotions. The leaders invited a different guest speaker each week, and each one had something different to offer. We do this in counselor training, cooking, crafts, and other electives. Be creative! Adapt to what you have in personnel and facilities. If your church does not have adequate room, you may be able to use some homes near the church for your small groups.

But to begin, you will need to think through your individual situation. This chapter is designed to help you and your committee correlate some of the things we have discussed in earlier chapters and to organize your thoughts and evaluations using the following simple outline. But note—it is just a suggestion. Be creative and add to it or expand it.

Design for _____
(Name of your church)

I. Prayer Group

Participants:

    Pastor's wife: _____

    Others: _____

    _____

    _____

    _____

Place: _____

Date: _____

Time: _____

Frequency: _____

Specific requests: _____

_____

Develop a sample survey: _____

II. Appointment with Your Pastor

Date: _____ Time: _____

Convey concerns: _____

_____

_____

_____

Request input: _____

_____

_____

Show him the sample survey: _____

_____

Request to survey: _____

    Date: _____

    Mechanics: _____

                    _____

Other suggested women: _____

                    _____

III. Refine and Finalize the Survey Form

Completion date: _____

Survey date: _____

Pastoral or other approval: _____

IV. Distribute Surveys and Compile Results

Develop a list of your greatest needs: _____

_____

_____

_____

_____

How can you meet those needs (develop goals)? _____

_____

_____

_____

_____

_____

V. Evaluation and Design of the New Program

What kind of program now exists? _____

_____

_____

_____

What kind of program are you recommending? _____

_____

_____

_____

Target date to begin: _____

How will you handle the following programming elements?

    Frequency: _____

    Day/Night: _____

    Child care: _____

    Finances: _____

    Leadership: _____

    Teaching: _____

    Recruitment: _____

    Presentation to church leadership: _____

_____

What board positions are needed to accomplish your goals? (Job descriptions are given in chapter 7.)

_____

_____

_____

Who will serve on your first Women's Ministries Board?

_____

_____

_____

Target date for presentation to leadership: _____

VI. Specific Plans to Move Ahead After Board Approval

Subject for the first series: _____

_____

Number of sessions: _____ Day of the week: _____

Time: _____ Bible teacher: _____

Electives to be offered: _____

_____

_____

_____

Brochure preparation for the series: _____

(See Appendix 4 for examples.) _____

_____

_____

The kind of kickoff event: (i.e., luncheon, coffee, dinner): _____

_____

The date and time for the kickoff event: _____

_____

VII. Kickoff Event for the New Program

Speaker who can motivate women ministering to women: _____

_____

Invite the pastor to welcome the women: _____

Posters: _____

Skits: _____

Other details: _____

_____

_____

Hand out brochures and answer questions: _____

_____

VIII. Conduct the First Series

Subject: _____ Bible teacher: _____

Dates: _____ Day and time: _____

_____

Hand out evaluation sheets: _____

IX. Evaluation and Appreciation of the First Series

Notes of appreciation to the participants: _____

Luncheon of appreciation for elective leaders: _____

Review surveys: _____

_____

_____

_____

Areas for improvement: _____

_____

_____

_____

New people who were involved: _____

_____

_____

_____

Potential leadership: _____

_____

_____

New series: _____

Bible teacher: _____

Dates: _____   Number of weeks: _____

Electives: _____

_____

_____

_____

Other: _____

_____

_____

_____

7
A Magazine of Resources

When we are planning a new project around the house or in the garden, most of us enjoy looking at magazines full of beautiful pictures and ideas. We get inspiration and stimulation from others for our own project. That is the purpose of this chapter. In it you will find detailed information concerning the various components of the Women's Ministries organization at Northwest Bible Church. The information is included not because we believe ours is the only way, or even the best way, but merely as an example of one way to set up a program.

We hope that these work sheets will give you inspiration and direction. But remember—we have been developing our program over the past seven years. Yours will take time also. Let the ideas in this chapter stimulate your thinking, and exercise creativity in adapting them for the unique situation in your own church.

First is included an organizational chart of our Women's Ministries Board. Then we have included complete job descriptions for each of the ten board positions.

The handout "Guidelines for Elective Leaders" is what we give each woman who is to lead one of the small elective groups.

Practical guidelines for planning special events such as retreats, luncheons, and "Saturday Specials" are included to help you capture the details needed to have a really organized event on your first try. We have also given you some ideas on how to handle the luncheons and suppers that end each session.

Next is a list of the various electives we have offered over the past seven years. Finally, we have included a list of all the outreach projects we have been involved with here in Dallas.

We hope that these guidelines will stimulate your group to even greater creativity.

Women's Ministries Board

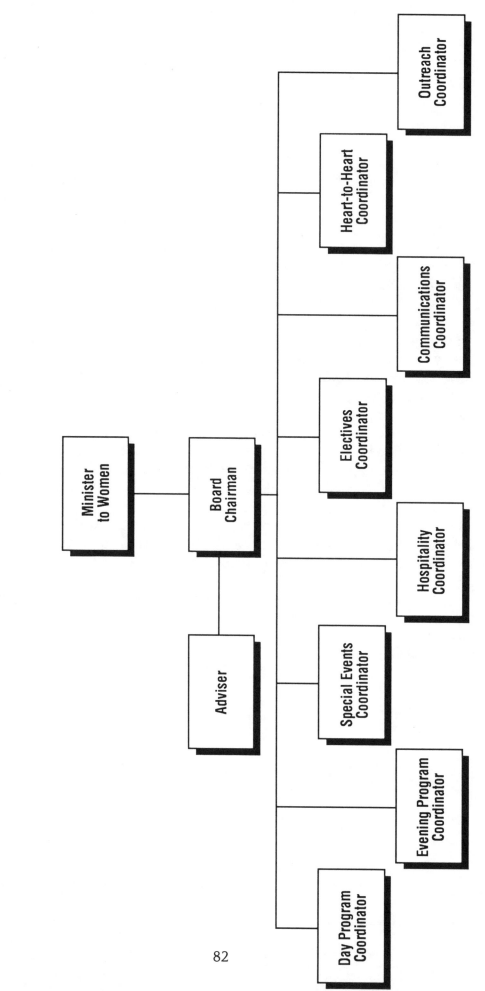

Job Descriptions
Minister to Women

Reporting relationship: The associate pastor and the elder board
Primary function: To oversee the Women's Ministries program

Responsibilities

Ministry to Women
1. Plan, promote, and coordinate weekly a Women's Ministries program for Tuesday mornings and Wednesday evenings (September–May)
2. Prepare and teach Bible lessons Tuesdays and Wednesdays
3. Meet regularly with the Women's Ministries Board
4. Assist members of the board in accomplishing their responsibilities
5. Recruit new Women's Ministries Board members
6. Recruit Bible teachers
7. Help recruit leaders for the elective classes.
8. Coordinate training for support counseling ministry
9. Carry out discipleship and leadership development
10. Provide personal counseling on request
11. Prepare and administer the Women's Ministries' budget
12. Speak to individual groups as requested, e.g., singles, young mothers, youth
13. Hospital visitation
14. Supervise women interns from Dallas Theological Seminary
15. Supervise and participate in the yearly retreat and other special events
16. Supervise "Saturday Specials" in the summer
17. Supervise and approve all ministries for women in the church and for women in the community, among which may be
    a. R.E.A.C.H., in cooperation with a Crisis Pregnancy Center
    b. Breast cancer support group
    c. Care-givers (lay counseling)
    d. Abortion recovery
    e. Homeless and battered women shelters
    f. Mom-to-Mom (young mothers' support)
    g. Professional women's group
    h. Widows' support group
18. Monthly Bible study with support staff women

Coordination with the staff and elder board
1. Attend weekly staff meetings
2. Report weekly to the associate pastor
3. Report in writing and in person to the elder board as requested.

Other responsibilities
1. Assist other churches in starting Women's Ministries programs, offering suggestions by phone, letter, and personal interviews.

2. Frequently speak in other church meetings and retreats
3. Visiting lecturer in the Women's Ministries course at Dallas Theological Seminary

Women's Ministries Board
Chairman

Reporting relationship: Minister to women
Primary function: To chair the Women's Ministries Board and to advise and assist the minister to women when the board is not in session

Responsibilities

1. Chair the meetings of the Women's Ministries Board
2. See that each member of the board is functioning in her area of responsibility
3. Plan the times and agendas of the meetings; arrange for recording the minutes of the meetings
4. Provide a calendar of events and meeting dates for each member
5. Be responsible for keeping the board informed between meetings
6. Meet regularly with the minister to women when the board is not in session
7. Plan the agendas for the Tuesday meetings and make announcements and/or prepare announcements to be given to elective leaders
8. Appoint a secretary to record the minutes of board meetings
9. Support and encourage others in their positions on the board

Day Program Coordinator

Reporting relationship: Chairman of the Women's Ministries Board
Primary function: To oversee the operation of the morning program

Responsibilities

1. See that the facility needs of the teachers are met as they have requested
2. See that the P.A. system is set up and manned and that all equipment is returned to its proper place
3. Work with the coordinator of electives to keep in regular contact with elective leaders
4. Write a personal thank-you note to each elective leader when her teaching period is over
5. Collect and keep a record of the offering and make a date/attendance/offering chart
6. Assist the minister to women in the selection of a pianist and leader of music (the songtime should be 9:30-9:40, with occasionally one additional song after the teacher speaks)

7. Collect and distribute the tape orders; appoint someone to sit in the foyer with tapes before and after the class to answer questions concerning the tapes
8. Take tapes, offering, and tape orders to the church office
9. Support and encourage others in their positions on the board

Evening Program Coordinator

Reporting Relationship: Chairman of the Women's Ministries Board
Primary function: To oversee the operation of the night program

Responsibilities

1. See that the facility needs of the teachers are met as they have requested
2. See that the P.A. equipment is set up and manned and that all equipment is returned to its proper place
3. Write a personal thank-you note to each elective leader when her teaching period is over
4. Assist the minister to women in the selection of a pianist and leader of music
5. Collect and distribute the tape orders
6. Be responsible for the refreshments on Wednesday evening, which could occasionally include more than coffee
7. Keep a written record of the number present each week, giving the number to the minister to women
8. Assist the hospitality coordinator at the end-of-session dinner
9. Be the "hostess" on Wednesday evenings, being present at the welcoming table to greet and assist ladies
10. Support and encourage others in their positions on the board

Outreach Coordinator

Reporting relationship: Chairman of the Women's Ministries Board
Primary function: To oversee existing outreach ministries and to organize and implement new ones as opportunities arise

Responsibilities

1. Submit the names of possible leaders for each outreach ministry to the minister to women for approval before recruiting them
2. Have the leader of each outreach ministry report to her and meet with or call her at least monthly to assist and to encourage
3. Investigate new ministries and report to the board on their feasibility for the church and update the board members at meetings
4. Be alert to opportunities that come up throughout the year that offer outreach participation

5. Coordinate the flow of information on outreach opportunities to the church and encourage participation through a variety of means: announcements, sign-up sheets, recruitment calls
6. Support and encourage others in their positions on the board

Committees for Outreach

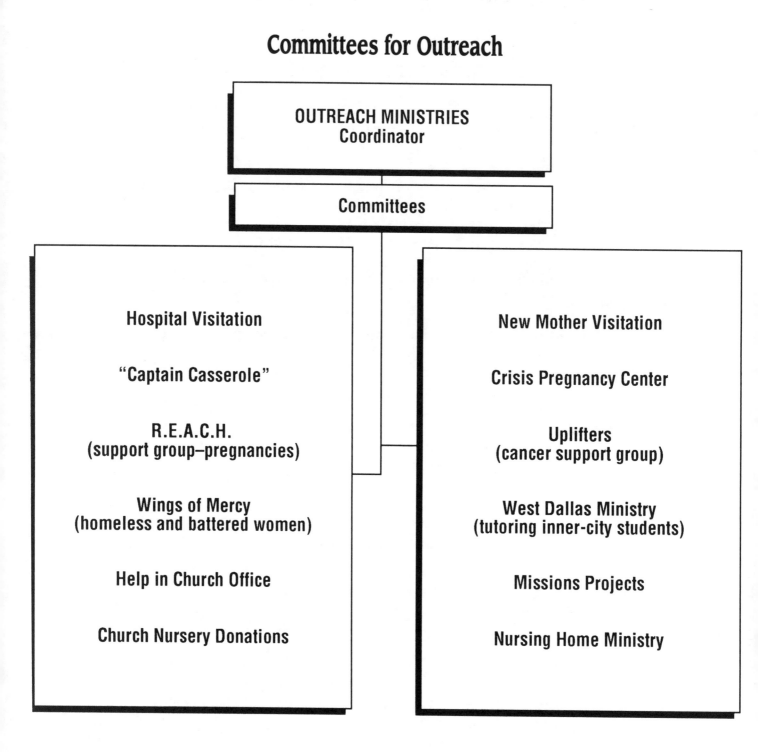

OUTREACH MINISTRIES
Coordinator

Committees

Hospital Visitation

"Captain Casserole"

R.E.A.C.H.
(support group–pregnancies)

Wings of Mercy
(homeless and battered women)

Help in Church Office

Church Nursery Donations

New Mother Visitation

Crisis Pregnancy Center

Uplifters
(cancer support group)

West Dallas Ministry
(tutoring inner-city students)

Missions Projects

Nursing Home Ministry

Hospitality Coordinator

Reporting Relationship: Chairman of the Women's Ministries Board
Primary function: To coordinate the activities involving hospitality

Responsibilities

1. Coordinate the day luncheon and the evening dinner with the night coordinator at the end of each session and select women to assist her
2. Assist the coordinator of special events where her responsibilities overlap with that of the hospitality coordinator
3. Be responsible for the refreshments on Tuesday morning, which could occasionally include more than coffee
4. Be responsible for the orientation meeting for the elective leaders
5. Be responsible for selecting gifts for the elective leaders at the end of each session
6. Coordinate the elective leaders' luncheon (table decoration and menu) during each session for the elective leaders
7. During each session, provide individual class luncheons with beverages; be prepared to inform elective leaders two weeks in advance
8. For board meetings, provide coffee, hot water and ice water, and possibly include simple snacks
9. Provide the menu and food for end-of-year board retreat
10. Provide the beverages and snacks for the "Saturday Specials"
11. Support and encourage others in their respective positions

Summary Overview

Each session
1. Orientation meeting
2. Individual class luncheons
3. Elective leaders' luncheons
4. Day lunch
5. Evening dinner
6. Elective leader gifts

Monthly
1. Board meetings

Once per year
1. Board retreat
2. "Saturday Specials"
3. Song leader and pianist gifts

Special Events Coordinator

Reporting relationship: Chairman of the Women's Ministries Board
Primary function: To be responsible for all special programs apart from the regular weekly program, such as retreats, luncheons, and seminars

Responsibilities

1. Select committees to assist in organizing the special events
2. Investigate potential programs and report to the Women's Ministries Board regarding their feasibility for us (the choice of the speaker shall

be a board decision)

3. As called upon, assist the hospitality coordinator where her responsibilities overlap with those of the special events coordinator
4. Work with the electives coordinator to enlist elective leaders for the "Saturday Specials"
5. Support and encourage others in their positions on the board

Electives Coordinator

Reporting Relationship: Chairman of the Women's Ministries Board
Primary function: To recruit elective leaders for each session and to act as a liaison between the Women's Ministries Board and elective leaders

Responsibilities

1. Seek out women from the church to share their talents with the Women's Ministries program
2. Coordinate electives each session in order to maintain variety and balance in the program
3. Obtain descriptions of electives from the elective leaders, prepare the brochure, and give it to the secretary to be printed
4. Assist the elective leaders in planning their room setup and in obtaining needed supplies, such as overhead projectors, a blackboard, recorders, and TV monitors, and give a list of those requirements to the secretary
5. Prior to each session, turn in room setup requirements to the secretary in charge of scheduling
6. Check to make sure that the room setup is correct
7. Contact and assess the needs of the elective leaders and communicate information from the board
8. Coordinate activities with the special events coordinator for the "Saturday Specials"
9. Contact elective leaders about luncheons and special information
10. Support and encourage others in their positions on the board

Communications and Child Care Coordinator

Reporting relationship: Chairman of the Women's Ministries Board
Primary function: To provide for the publicity needs of the Women's Ministries program and for child care during all Women's Ministries functions

Responsibilities

1. Determine the number of children in the program and communicate that information to the person in charge of the nursery
2. Report back to the Women's Ministries Board concerning any needs that may arise

3. Oversee the functioning of the child care program during Women's Ministries functions
4. Be responsible for any promotion, such as posters, special fliers, or newspaper announcements, for regular activities and/or special events
5. Be responsible for placing notices in the church bulletin
6. Support and encourage others in their positions on the board

Heart-to-Heart Coordinator

Reporting Relationship: Chairman of the Women's Ministries Board
Primary function: To oversee the operation of the Heart-to-Heart ministry of Senior and Junior partners

Responsibilities

1. Select an assistant to help with administrative responsibilities
   a. To help in matchintg Senior/Junior partners
   b. To help make rematches when necessary
   c. To help coordinate and publicize social events
2. Select the Senior and Junior members for the Heart-to-Heart steering committee
   a. To call the matched partners for followup and accountability
   b. To assist in preparing for coffees, teas, social events, and announcements
3. As able, assist other churches in starting Heart-to-Heart programs
4. Support and encourage others in their positions on the board

Suggestions for Securing Elective Leaders

All the members of the Women's Ministries Board are continually listening to program participants and seeking new and beneficial types of electives as well as suggesting women who would be able to lead them. So personal contacts and recommendations are probably our most frequently used method for securing elective leaders.

Also, at the close of each session of the Women's Ministries program we take a survey, such as the one on page 91, providing an opportunity both for suggestions as well as volunteers to help teach. This provides an entry point for new people to participate in a more significant way if they would like to. The board then considers these possibilities and acts as a clearing house to decide exactly what will be offered and who will lead.

Some women would be comfortable sharing a skill such as sewing or cooking, but would not be comfortable leading the prayer and sharing aspect of the elective. In such cases we have found it most helpful to pair that woman with another woman who would handle those functions. As she works as a team, many times the woman who was initially hesitant to lead the prayer and sharing becomes much more confident and develops in a new area herself. Elective leadership is an excellent training ground for future leaders of the Women's Ministries program.

Some electives, such as an elective concerning family devotions, cooking, or training in lay counseling, might be too varied in content to expect from only one teacher. In those cases we have found it effective to invite a different speaker for each of the six to eight sessions, with different women sharing their experiences. In our counselor training elective, for instance, that has allowed us to have professional counselors come and add their expertise without having to be there each week. When you have different speakers, however, it is important to have one woman who is the facilitator for the whole session. She meets with all the other elective leaders and handles the shepherding aspects of the elective class. This provides the valuable link of communication between the board and this class.

Women's Ministries Electives Survey

Please take the time to tell us what you'd like to have offered for the fall session.

We NEED your input, ideas, and feedback!

I attend _____ Tuesday morning _____ Wednesday evening _____

What things do you particularly like about the Women's Ministries program?

_____

_____

Is there anything you'd like to see changed about the Women's Ministries program or its format?

_____

_____

Do you have a skill or talent that you could share with or teach to other women?

1. _____   2. _____

What other elective courses would you like to see taught?

1. _____   2. _____

Listed below are some of the classes that have been requested or suggested. Please indicate if you would be willing to teach or team teach any of them.

_____ Gardening	_____ Needlework/crafts
_____ Floral arranging	_____ Blended families
_____ Oil/folk art painting	_____ Dealing with stress
_____ Home economy	_____ Ministry of encouragement
_____ Loss and the grief process	_____ Spiritual accountability

Ways I could help

_____ Pass out songbooks	_____ Take offering
_____ Lead singing	_____ Work on retreat
_____ Play piano	_____ You name it, I'm willing

Do you have any constructive suggestions that might improve the effectiveness of the Women's Ministries program?

_____

_____

Name _____   Address _____

Phone _____   Church home _____

Is there a retreat speaker you could recommend? _____

Would you be interested in a retreat in a Dallas area hotel? _____

Guidelines for Elective Leaders

The elective is an integral part of the entire program. It is not only the means of communicating a skill, but also the means of drawing people together in smaller groups to encourage their spiritual growth. For this reason an elective leader must consider herself not only a teacher, but also a role model.

Plan to arrive by 9:15 A.M. on Tuesdays and 6:30 P.M. on Wednesdays so that you can be present for the beginning of the Bible study. This is the primary event of each session. Your presence will be a means of personal blessing and will also indicate to others its importance to you.

1. Call the people on your list and tell them they are in your class and where you will be meeting. Give them necessary preliminary information.
2. Keep an attendance record. Call absentees to let them know they were missed.
3. Arrange now for a substitute who can be available on short notice. If you know you cannot be there on a specific date, arrange for a teacher ahead of time.
4. Choose a class hostess. She can help you welcome people, keep in touch with absentees, and clean up afterwards. She can also help you keep track of time so that the first or last fifteen minutes can be spent in sharing and prayer.
5. Suggest that each person keep her name tag in her Bible or purse. Encourage the use of the name tags each week for everyone's sake.
6. The sharing time is important for the development of relationships. Be ready with a prayer request or praise if starting is slow. That will encourage others. You may vary the format. Pray conversationally at the end, or have someone pray immediately as each request is given. Be careful of time-hogs. Do not skimp on this time. It is essential for the spiritual growth of the group.
7. Members of the Women's Ministries Board will sometimes visit different classes. The board is always available to help. (Here we provide a list of the names and phone numbers of the Women's Ministries Board.)

Planning a Women's Retreat

I. Plan ahead

A. One year
  1. Visit and reserve the retreat center
  2. Board selects speaker

B. Four to six months ahead
  1. Select a theme that complements the speaker's topics
  2. Select committee chairmen
     a. Publicity
     b. Registration
     c. Cabin hostesses
     d. Serendipity
     e. Skits/Entertainment
     f. Music
     g. Free time activities

C. Two months ahead
   1. Contact the speaker, have her send a photograph for publicity, and, if desired, have her prepare questions for small group follow-up discussion
   2. Begin publicity

D. Four weeks ahead
   1. Begin registration
   2. Prepare an information booklet that includes such things as the schedule, fellowship group questions, a map of retreat center, Saturday free time activities, an appreciation page, and space for notes
   3. Purchase gifts for the committee chairmen

II. Divide the responsibility: Committee job descriptions

A. Publicity
   1. Design and make arrangements for flyers, bulletins, and so on
   2. Contact Sunday school classes with announcements
   3. Make and display posters

B. Registration
   1. Design and distribute forms
   2. Collect money and registrations
   3. Make room assignments following requests on the forms for first and second choices (some dorms may be indicated as "Early" or "Late" for those who prefer either)
   4. Mail letter to registrants with detailed information
   5. Have registration set up at camp
   6. Provide packets and name tags
   7. Make scholarships available
   8. Give the bottom of registration form to the carpool committee

C. Cabin hostesses
   1. Set the mood for cabin, welcome guests
   2. Be at camp early with table setup
   3. Set up the table for coffee and hot water for tea
   4. Use the table decorations that will come from the serendipity committee
   5. Provide each hostess with two coffee pots and coffee (regular and decaf)
   6. Keep the hostess table neat at all times

D. Serendipity
   1. Provide table arrangements for the dorm hostesses, dining room, and speaker's room
   2. Bring pillow surprises and a gift for each woman (mints, bookmark, magnet)
   3. Make dorm, chapel, and dining room decorations

E. Skits/Entertainment
   1. Coordinate a special welcome for the first session using skits, singing, props, and/or mixers
   2. Plan for Saturday night; possibilities include talent show, takeoff of popular musicals, competitive skits

93

F. Music coordinator
1. Select a song leader and a pianist
2. Select people to do special music at each session (solos, duets, instrumentals)
3. Bring songbooks or overhead transparencies

G. Free time activities
1. Select people to facilitate/lead four free time activities
2. Publicize free time activities prior to the retreat
3. Provide registration for the activities and collect any costs
4. Arrange with the retreat center for appropriate space for activities and help set up for them at the retreat

Planning a Special Luncheon

I. Purpose is to provide an opportunity for women to

A. Participate in an all-women's function and to be exposed to the Women's Ministries program
B. Bring friends and family to be presented with the gospel message

II. Planning ahead

A. Six months: Select the speaker (Women's Ministries Board)
B. Two to four months: Select the theme to be used for publicity and throughout the luncheon; contact the speaker to discuss her topic and to ask for photographs for publicity.
C. Two months: Select committee chairmen
D. Two to three weeks: Pass around sign-up sheets to recruit help for the kitchen and decorating committees the day before the luncheon
E. One week: Send postcard reminder to all helpers
F. Day of luncheon: Recognize and thank all committees and helpers; give a small thank-you gift (e.g., a Christmas ornament at Christmas)

III. Committee job descriptions

A. Publicity
1. Design invitations, tickets, and posters
2. Make arrangements with the communications coordinator for announcements, bulletins, and other church-wide publications

B. Menu
1. Consider the limitations of hot vs. cold menu items; make a decision based on number of people served
2. Have the menu coordinate with the theme when possible
3. Work with the food service to order and prepare the food, or have it catered

C. Decorations
1. Set up a welcome table including name tags, flowers, and centerpieces
2. Provide centerpieces for tables
3. Coordinate decorations for the stage/platform area

D. Music
1. Select a song leader
2. Select a piano player
3. Select someone to do special music
4. Have taped music or a pianist playing while people arrive

Planning a Heart-to-Heart Tea

At Northwest Bible church the Heart-to-Heart committee gives an annual after-noon tea. We schedule it for the first Friday of March at 2:00 P.M. and call it "Tea at Two." We invite all the women who regularly attend our church. Reservations are necessary for proper planning. We also provide nursery for children kindergarten age and younger.

This tea accomplishes several goals. First, it helps to publicize the Heart-to-Heart ministry in a nonpressured atmosphere. We offer material, have a Senior share her testimony, and provide an occasion where younger and older women are together en-joying each other's company. This is not a sign-up time! However, we find that many Seniors join the following fall after having had the summer months to think over all they heard and experienced at the tea.

Second, the tea provides a delightful atmosphere for partners to enjoy each other's company. It also gives the committee a special opportunity to serve our women loving-ly and graciously. When the women come, they feel they are a part of a ministry that cares deeply about them. Furthermore, there is something wonderful about going to an event that is lovely and completely feminine. Our hope is that this time of fellowship and spiritual encouragement will enhance the joy of being a Christian woman.

During the tea we always have a guest speaker share her testimony, give a book review, or relate an experience of great spiritual growth and dependence upon God. There are certainly other topics of interest that could be covered. We are simply careful not to duplicate the style of our weekly Bible study. Our women have been deeply touched by these Heart-to-Heart teas, and several guests have trusted Christ as Savior.

Our women love the Heart-to-Heart Tea and look forward to it each year. Yes, it does require time and detailed planning, but it also is fun! Be creative, read books on formal and informal teas, and involve your women. We were surprised when we real-ized we were teaching many young women hospitality skills. We were also happy to see what a bonding experience working on such a project can be among women. Most of all, keep an attitude of loving service during all of your preparations, and pray that all will be done for God's glory.

Room Preparations and Table Settings

Round tables for guests
Tables for coffee, tea, and food
White tablecloths
Podium
Piano
Table for name tags and informational materials
Taping and sound system
Floral arrangements or centerpieces
Two silver services
Two extra coffee pots for quick replenishing
Two crystal or silver water pitchers
Four white linen cloths for holding under pitchers
Extra silver trays for food
Several candelabra and long white candles
China cups and plates
Doilies, white and lacy
Water glasses
Spoons, forks
Napkins, folded
Two spoons or tongs for sugar
Crystal or china dish for lemon slices
Crystal bowl for mints
(Many of these items can be rented, if necessary)

Responsibilities

Food planning
Name tags
Heart-to-Heart information
Flowers
Pianist
Senior testimony and speaker
Tea server
Coffee server
Greeters
Replenish tea and coffee
Replenish food
Bulletin announcements
Group reminders or invitations
Letter invitations to the matched partners
Nursery arrangements
Sunday School announcements
Honorarium or gift for the speaker and the pianist

FOOD SUGGESTIONS FOR THE TEA

Coffee, Tea, and Treats

Gourmet coffee (e.g., Vanilla Praline)
Gourmet tea (Passion Blend or fruit)
Iced water with lemon slices and mint leaves
Lemon slices (stuck with cloves in middle) for tea table
Cream, really *milk,* for tea and coffee
Sugar, lump or granulated, for tea and coffee
Buttered mints on tea and coffee tables

Food Ideas

Portions are small, dainty morsels
Tea sandwiches—crusts always removed
    slivered ham
    slice of cucumber or watercress with herbed butter
    cream cheese with date nut bread
Lemon pound cake
Pear or apple cake
Pumpkin nut bread or muffins
Lemon thyme bread
Milk and honey bread with honey butter
Hot mini-muffins
Sponge cake with layer of strawberry jam and whipped cream
Cream cakes
Small cheesecakes with raspberries or kiwi on top
Fruitcake squares
Scones with preserves and whipped cream
Shortbreads
Crumpets
Cookies, wafers
"Petite madeleines"
Lemon squares
Petits fours
Fancy pastries
Jam tarts
Chocolate-covered strawberries or dried apricots
Fresh fruit

Schedule

10:30 Begin setting up, folding napkins, etc.
        Food can be delivered until 1:30
        Pray together
 1:30 Instruct servers
        Check room

1:45 Bring out food and drinks
1:50 Be ready! Piano playing, ready to greet and serve for early birds
2:00 1. Greet, give name tags, offer Heart-to-Heart book
      2. Guide to food tables, plates with doilies
      3. Guide to coffee (always on the side of the table closest to entrance) or tea (always on the side of the table farthest from entrance); spoons on drink tables
      4. Guests find table and friends; each table has folded beautiful napkins, forks, and floral centerpiece
2:35 Announce that guests have two more minutes before the program begins
2:37 Welcome warmly (chairman)
      Introduce Senior
2:39 Senior testimony
2:42 Introduce speaker
2:43 Speaker begins
3:15 Speaker finishes
3:16 Chairman thanks the speaker and guests for coming; she invites the guests to return for more refreshments
3:30 Nursery closes, tea officially ends
3:50 Tea *really* ends; clean up
4:30 Go home and collapse!

Planning a "Saturday Special"

I. Purpose: To provide an opportunity for women to

A. Keep in touch during the summer months
B. Be exposed to the Women's Ministries program if they have not participated
C. Bring friends and family to be presented with the gospel message

II. Responsibilities of the special events coordinator

A. Have the board select speakers and dates
B. Work with the elective coordinator to select four diverse electives and appropriate leaders
C. Have elective leaders give descriptions, costs, and class sizes for the brochure
D. Determine if participants will bring sack lunches or if the event will be catered
E. Design the registration brochure and have the communications coordinator take care of additional publicity
F. Start registration three to four weeks in advance

Creative Meal Planning Suggestions

We have found it helpful to incorporate a good deal in planning the meal that completes each of our sessions of the Women's Ministries program. The daytime program closes with a luncheon; the evening program concludes with a supper.

Sometimes we ask that everyone bring a salad or a dessert. We have found it helpful to limit the desserts to two per elective class. We provide the drinks.

Other times we order something like quiche from a bakery, or we make a couple of pans of lasagna. Then the board will prepare a salad and finger desserts.

Another thing we have enjoyed is to buy ingredients for a taco salad. We charge a small amount to cover costs (e.g., $3.00 per person). The board and volunteers come the day before to set up and decorate the tables.

When we plan a supper for the evening session, we find it most convenient to provide the meal and charge a small amount as above. The women don't mind bringing desserts. They especially enjoy the opportunity to eat together in a relaxed atmosphere.

We try to keep variety in our planning and menu, for we know that creates greater anticipation and enjoyment—and having the tables decorated, even very simply, provides a feminine and festive atmosphere.

Elective Class Suggestions

Skill Development

Counted Cross Stitch
English Smocking
Knitting
Country Crafts
Quilting
Stenciling
Crocheted Vests
Calligraphy
Flower Arrangements
Collars and Sweats
Needlepoint
Crocheted Heart Rug
Christmas Crafts
Painted House Firescreen
Cover It with Fabric
Craft Potpourri
Knitted Sweatshirts and Fabric Tee Shirts
Needle Knows
Finishing Touch (women bring their own projects to complete here)

Christian Life

Scripture Memory
Training in Evangelism/Discipleship
Lay Support Counseling Training
Discipleship as a Lifestyle
Prayer: Key to Spiritual Fitness
Fundamentals of Biblical Counseling
Missions Out There Somewhere?

How to Study the Bible on Your Own
Behold Your God
Bible Study Follow-up
A Look at 1 Peter
Attributes of God in Exodus
New Age Movement
Pursuing the Power of Prayer
Remedial Quiet Time 101
Living the Reality of What Christ Began
One Bold Voice and Two Shaky Knees (adult evangelism)
Planting Productive Seed (child evangelism)
Praying for Character Qualities in One Another

Family Helps

Nutrition: Key to a Healthy Family
Tennis
Aerobics
Time Management and Home Organization
Hospitality at Your Home
The Hows of Home Education
Parenting Principles for the Difficult Years
Motherhood: Not a Job for Sissies
Chinese Cooking
Cake Decorating
Self Image
CPR
Microwave Cooking
So You're Not Betty Crocker
Beyond Chicken Soup and Castor Oil
The Career of Homemaking
Kidding Around with Kids
Legal Matter Chatter
Good Grief
Home Sweet Home
Do the Most with What You Have
In Search of the Lost Art (homemaking)
Forever Lovely
Nutrition Concerns of Women
Weight Management
Christian Dating: The Single Dilemma
Things They Never Told You in Childbirth Class
Changing Lives Through Encouragement
Coping With Codependency
How to Remember to Remember
Responsible Financial Stewardship
Decorative Designs
All About Aging
Sibling Without Rivalry

Parenting Adult Children
Guiding Your Children's Sexual Values
Disciplining Children
Ministry of Encouragement

Outreach Ministries

Outreach to the Homeless

One year we ministered through the Dallas Life Foundation (a downtown shelter for the homeless) by collecting and delivering used clothing, household items, toiletries, and personal items. We also furnished Bibles and hymnals, held a weekly women's Bible study and a monthly birthday party, as well as collected grocery receipts for a computer.

Later, we supported a shelter for battered women and children by collecting clothing and household items for their thrift store, by holding a Tuesday morning shower for baby formula, diapers, and other items needed for a newborn, and by implementing an evangelistic birthday party for Jesus.

Currently we are supplying needs (irons, ironing boards, cleaning supplies) for a new homeless shelter. We are also showing the *Jesus* film as an evangelistic outreach and are combining efforts with our Men's Ministry, which is painting the outside of the building.

R.E.A.C.H.

This ministry offers support to women who are facing crisis pregnancies. It is a tangible way to be involved in providing an alternative to abortion for women who have unwanted pregnancies. Seeking to encourage the women emotionally and spiritually, the R.E.A.C.H. ministry maintains an ongoing relationship with the women. Participants call their clients, take them to doctor's appointments, and help them locate needed services. They sometimes accompany the clients to childbirth classes and occasionally to the delivery room. The R.E.A.C.H. group collects maternity, baby and young children's clothing, and baby furnishings.

Crisis Pregnancy Center (CPC)

This Christian ministry is dedicated to assisting women who come to them with an unplanned pregnancy. It offers practical, constructive alternatives to abortion and helps meet the emotional, practical, and spiritual needs of the mother. We encourage the training of our women to become counselors in Crisis Pregnancy Center offices, to answer abortion hot lines, to baby-sit, or to help this ministry in any way. We also support the CPC in our area with a monthly financial gift.

Abortion Recovery

The purpose of this ministry is to become a Good Samaritan to those who have been hurt by abortion. Through a ten-week Bible study, the women served by this ministry are shown how God sees abortion and through the group time learn how to experience God's forgiveness and grace. Some of these women then give their testimonies to encourage others to find healing.

West Dallas Ministry

Some of our women participate in a tutoring program that gives personal encouragement as well as academic tutoring in an inner-city housing community. This program is offered as an elective in the weekly Women's Ministries program. Volunteers car pool to the high school and meet with students on a one-to-one basis. The women pray together for their students immediately after the students return to class. This program continues even when the Women's Ministries program is not in session. Its purpose is to provide role models for character development and to encourage students to graduate from high school and to pursue further educational opportunities.

Hospital Visitation Committee

This group brings spiritual encouragement to women who are ill or have had surgery. Hospital or home visits are also made to women who have close family members in the hospital. Depending upon the individual situation, the committee members send cards, make telephone calls, and take food to the homes of the women served by this ministry.

Captain Casserole

This committee was begun to utilize leftover food from our Wednesday night dinners at church. Volunteers prepare supplemental casseroles in disposable containers, which are then stored in the church freezer. This food is available for people who have an illness in the family, for new mothers, or for anyone in our church who needs help with meals.

New Mothers

This committee ministers to women in our church body who have recently welcomed new babies into their homes, either by birth or by adoption. Our purpose is to show support and encouragement by a personal visit either at the hospital or at home. We have taken such little gifts as the Golden Book *Prayers for Children,* or a calligraphy print of Psalm 127:3. This year we are giving the new mothers a packet of verses that relate to mothering and child rearing to encourage memorization.

Welcoming Newcomers Group

This committee receives the visitors' cards from the church office and calls the women. They welcome them to the church and inform them about the Women's Ministries program as well as answer any questions they may have about other church activities.

Help in Church Office

These volunteers are available when the church office has special projects or large mailings that require extra hands.

Citizens' Awareness Table

This table, which is available at the Women's Ministries sessions, is a source of information about local, state, and national issues. Through it, women are encouraged to become involved in the political process by taking action that can make a difference. Such actions include contacting their elected representative by letter, phone, or in person; writing letters to the editors of newspapers; and, especially, being an informed voter.

Parent-to-Parent

This is a preventative drug education workshop for parents of elementary age and older children; it is available through Pride Parent Training, (813)393-9878. Two women in our church received their facilitator training and held workshops targeting sixth through twelfth graders. We encouraged all the women in our Women's Ministries program to (1) consider becoming a facilitator, and (2) encourage their children's school to offer the workshop for the parents there.

Sharing Closet

The purpose of this closet is to meet the needs of our missionaries who are home on furlough, of members of our church, and of other needy people. Examples of items collected are gently worn clothing, household items, and, if you have the room, furniture in good repair.

Special Missions Projects

One ongoing project is the tape ministry. Our weekly Bible lessons are taped and sent worldwide to our women missionaries. Other projects have included making individual prayer cards about missionaries, sewing mosquito nets for missionaries in Africa, making wordless books and bean bags for child evangelism clubs, providing financial support for short-term missionaries, donating clothes and money for Bibles for Romania, and giving money for materials for our men's and high school ministries to build houses for widows in Guatemala.

We are presently providing financial support so that a sister church in Austria can provide Bibles for refugee families and starter kits for homemaking when the refugees find an apartment.

Twelve Step Study Group

This group meets once a week to encourage and support one another in changing codependent behaviors into emotionally healthy lifestyles in order to serve the Lord more effectively. We use *The Twelve Steps: A Spiritual Journey* (San Diego: Recovery) as our guide. (See Appendix 5 for a suggested reading list.)

Support Group for Children with Special Needs

A parent who has a child with special needs volunteered to organize a Sunday school class for children of all ages who might not benefit from regular classes.

Mom-to-Mom

This group evolved out of an elective that encouraged mothers with young children. The group meets once a month during the school year, invites appropriate speakers, has a picnic for moms and their kids in June, plans a Valentine's Day dinner for moms and dads, maintains a prayer chain, and helps decorate the church nursery by painting bright murals. Experienced moms in our church are also invited to meet with them to share their wisdom.

Evening Bible Study for Business and Professional Women

This Bible study ministers to working women. The group meets at the church to help the women deal with the special problems women encounter in the workplace and to apply scriptural principles to them.

Uplifters

This support group functions as an outreach to women dealing with breast cancer. Emphasis is placed on a one-to-one relationship where family and personal needs can be met. The Uplifters arrange annually for the mammography mobile unit to be at the church for two days (the same days that the main Women's Ministries sessions are held), and they handle the scheduling of appointments.

CanSupport

A support group for women who have cancer or for those who are caregivers for someone with cancer, CanSupport meets monthly at noon. The group keeps in touch between meetings with phone calls and lunches, thereby maintaining an atmosphere of faith and caring. They provide spiritual and prayer support while ministering to one another in practical ways.

Widows' Support Group (Hand-in-Hand)

This group provides help as new widows cope with their grief and opportunities for fellowship through regular meetings and interesting field trips. The group has put together a packet of information that a new widow should have. When a woman is newly widowed, one of its members is assigned to her and personally ministers to her. They also meet monthly for Sunday dinner in a restaurant and plan occasional outings for fellowship.

Other Possibilities

Ministry to Nursing Homes

This outreach group could obtain the names of those from their church in nursing homes and then visit, taking small remembrances, such as flowers, cards, or cookies. Other ideas include having your women present special music or lead craft projects and Bible studies.

Adopt a Grandparent

This ministry might include visits in the home, taking an older person out for meals occasionally, or any other thoughtful gesture to brighten the life an an older person.

Divorce Recovery Group

This group could provide support and encouragement for women facing the major adjustments that take place following a divorce. It possibly could include women whose adult children are experiencing divorce.

8
A Special Garden: Heart-to-Heart

What Is Heart-to-Heart?

A program that has been most successful here at Northwest in developing the important and supportive friendships between older and younger women (the "Seniors" and the "Juniors") is one we call "Heart-to-Heart." Because women understand women, have gone through similar experiences, and feel the same emotions, they can provide sympathetic listening and godly counsel and can often defuse tense situations before they escalate into major crises.

These spiritually mature women provide a biblical perspective of life, with their sound working knowledge of the Scriptures and a solid track record of godly conduct.

The experience, empathy, maturity, and spirituality of these women create an enormously powerful reservoir of untapped, God-given strength from which the church can benefit. Women need it; Scripture commands it. The Heart-to-Heart program taps this reservoir.

A Heart-to-Heart program can be initiated in any way that suits your church, consistent with its size and your culture. Informal gatherings, such as coffees or brunches, can be used to kick off the program, enabling women to meet each other and quickly establish areas of common interest. The general women's meetings, Sunday school classes, and worship services should be used for recruiting participants. We give each woman a profile sheet (which is included at the end of this chapter) to fill out to facilitate matching. We try to match women who have at least two interests in common and who are geographically close. That is particularly important in a metropolitan area.

Here are some guidelines we have found effective to develop a meaningful relationship.

- Make a one-year commitment to the relationship
- Contact each other once a week and meet at least once a month
- Pray for each other regularly
- Do things together (whether it be Bible study, shopping, learning a new skill, or just going to lunch; each set of partners is free to do what they want as long as they work on developing the relationship)

This ministry works. Some older women enjoy it so much that they are meeting with several younger women. And younger women love these friendships. They feel loved and have someone to call on for support and wisdom. As mentioned earlier, the isolation and loneliness women are feeling is not so much that the communication between *men and women* has broken down, but that the communication between *women and women* has broken down. Women need other women. Heart-to-Heart provides that contact.

This ministry is primarily a ministry of encouragement. It is not necessarily a formal discipleship program, nor is this an in-depth counseling service, but rather it is friendship for support, guidance, love, and encouragement. In addition, we ask that the partners pray with each other, for through prayer we can truly begin to understand the heart of the other woman and can experience the presence of God in our developing relationships.

We have found that there are several different reasons why Juniors are interested in this program. First, we have found that approximately 50 percent of our young women come from broken homes; therefore, they are seeking role-modeling from women who can give them hope and confidence that lifelong marriage is possible. Others want encouragement and advice on how to live with purity and integrity in their single and/or professional lives. Many have come to know the Lord, but they weren't reared in godly homes, and they don't know what a godly woman is like.

We also have many who have moved from out of town and miss their former support system of older women. One of our twenty-five-year-old women related how much she not only missed her mom, but her mom's friends and her friends' moms. She explained that when she first attended our women's ministries program she observed our women and thought, "These are such women-women, and I am such a girl-woman! How will I ever attain the maturity I see in them?"

As you might expect, she was the first to sign up for Heart-to-Heart that year, and has been greatly blessed by her new friendships.

Of course, we have mature and immature young women who simply enjoy the company and the friendship of an older woman who has a godly perspective and who has just lived a little longer. In fact, those are the credentials that we stress to our older or senior women. We emphasize what an opportunity God has given them to share what He has taught them throughout their lives. They have experienced joyful times as well as trials and heartaches, and they have always found God real and sufficient. They have practical knowledge from experience and have a God-given nurturing quality that is wonderfully developed.

As they experience this nurturing and warmth, many young women find it easier or safer to share their fears and insecurities with an older woman than with their peers. Furthermore, older women have a unique ability to comfort that younger women find to be special.

Win Couchman describes a mentoring relationship in this way:

> On Christmas Eve, a deep San Francisco-style fog kept our car crawling blindly along the road. Suddenly another car pulled onto the road right ahead of us. Because we were now following a set of beautiful twin taillights, we could safely increase our speed from fifteen to twenty-five miles per hour. A mentor is someone farther on down the road from you, who is going where you want to go, and who

is willing to give you some light to help you get there![1]

Older women have much to share. They will become true friends to the younger women. Yet this is a two-way street. The younger women will be ministering and caring for the older women as well. The focus will be to encourage one another to depend upon God, not upon the relationship. Therefore, the Bible, not just personal experiences, is to be the standard and authority.

The Heart-to-Heart program can be started in any size church. Your older women may need to be encouraged to accept the role of Seniors because generally they have not recognized the true value of their maturity and life experience. Those are their credentials for this relationship. The Heart-to-Heart program can become a source of healing, strength, and growth as these spiritually mature women are given meaningful influence in the lives of other women.

When women's unique needs are met by these godly role models, the entire church will be blessed.

How to Start

Administration

The Heart-to-Heart coordinator is a Women's Ministries Board member, and her primary function is to oversee the operation of the Heart-to-Heart Ministry of Senior and Junior partners.

Her responsibilities are listed in the job descriptions of the Women's Ministries Board.

The coordinator needs the valuable help of an assistant. She needs someone with whom to brainstorm and speak confidentially. The two women need to share in prayer and seek each other's wisdom, especially when making matches.

The chairman and the assistant chairman should use their knowledge of the women as well as the profile sheets to make matches. If possible, they should match women who live close to one another, and who have at least two interests or needs in common.

There should be an appropriate age span between the partners. Generally, women under thirty-five are Juniors, women between thirty-five and forty-five are either, and women forty-five and over are Seniors. Some women in the late twenties and thirties can become a Senior to a very young woman, but also become a Junior to an older woman. Just be careful not to become too rigid with age guidelines. One year, for example, we had a twenty-one year old, who was still in college and had been married only two months, sign up. We were able to match her with a twenty-nine year old who had been married eight years, had a seven-year-old daughter, and who in terms of experience and spiritual maturity was able to minister to her new, younger friend. On the other hand, we matched a fifty-one-year-old woman, who was a new believer and who

---

1. Win Couchman, "Cross-Generational Relationships," lecture to Women for Christ, 1983 Winter Break (tape available from Domain Communications, Wheaton, Illinois, 60187).

had just been married for the first time, with a godly seventy-year-old widow who had enjoyed a long and wonderful marriage.

Know that the more you study the interests, ages, personalities, and spiritual maturity of your women, the better your matches are going to be. Most of all, *pray!* We never match unless we have peace about it. We have seen how the Lord has put women together for reasons we could never have known previously.

When a match is made, the Senior partner should initiate the first call to her Junior, but from then on calling should be equal between the two.

The steering committee consists of trustworthy Junior and Senior women who serve two-year terms. They are each given a list of matches that they are responsible to pray for and to call monthly. The Juniors and Seniors are called alternately through the year; therefore, each woman is called bimonthly in order to see if she and her partner have met and if the relationship is going well. The partners' general comments are then recorded in the committee members' card file.

In our calling, we must be careful not to offend by treating women as though they were children, and we must use common sense. When calling, for example, have something to inform that woman about, such as an upcoming church luncheon or tea that would be fun to attend with her partner. If you have seen a woman and she has told you about her Junior-Senior relationship, there is no reason to call her. But in general, plan on calling the women, because your calling helps provide accountability and helps your women feel special, cared for, and part of a larger whole of committed and growing women.

The committee member may discuss ideas with a partner, but any problem or confidential matter should be immediately referred to the coordinator. If the problem is severe, the coordinator should seek help from her authority within the Women's Ministries program.

The most common difficulty is one of overcommitment. Often when a match is not working, inquiry by the committee person will find that one of the partners is too busy. Give the partner a graceful out and remake the match.

The coordinator and assistant coordinator should call their steering committee members monthly to find out how the matches are progressing. The coordinator should also keep a file of profile sheets, brochures, entertainment records, and suggestions.

Timing

We have found that September or October is the optimum time for signing up for Heart-to-Heart, but you may choose a month more convenient for your situation. Women's lives, especially those with children, tend to run on a school calendar. Plan to publicize and sign up for an entire month.

As much as possible try to limit your matches to that month, rather than trying as we did at first to match people all year long. You could make exceptions, but it does complicate the program as it grows. After your matching is completed, have a potluck lunch. It will be fun, and the gathering will help get your partners started.

In addition, we are now giving a spring tea to attract Seniors to the program. This is not a sign-up time, but rather a lovely opportunity to enjoy the fellowship of women of all ages. This event gives women several months to consider what they have heard so that they will be better prepared to make a commitment in the fall.

We were delighted to discover other benefits of giving a tea. First, it provides another way for us to say "We love you" to our women through serving them. Second, it makes our women feel special and feminine, and it teaches them hospitality. Finally, it gives our women a nonthreatening place to bring friends who do not know Christ personally.

Publicity

1. Spend the month of September advertising
   a. Make announcements and provide information and sign-up tables throughout the church
   b. Place announcements in the church bulletins and newsletters
2. Host a sign-up coffee
   a. Give one on a Saturday to accommodate women working outside the home (nursery can be provided at church)
   b. Coffees preferably should be held in a committee member's home; committee members should provide the food, juice, and coffee
   c. Provide name tags, profile sheets, and Heart-to-Heart brochures
   d. The coordinator or her assistant should initiate a time of group sharing during which the concept and commitment of Heart-to-Heart is presented; the coordinator should also encourage group interaction by presenting two or three self-revealing questions from which each chooses one to share with the group
   e. Ascertain if any women present wish to be matched together
3. Give a Heart-to-Heart tea (see chapter 7 for more information)
4. Pass the word along! Encourage partners to tell others how wonderful the program is and how God has used it to minister to them

Common Questions for Problem Solving

Question:

What if there are not enough older women in your church?

Answer:

Until your church attracts more older women or until your women grow older, ask your spiritually mature women in their thirties to serve as seniors. Then inform your unmatched Juniors that you will match them as soon as a Senior is available.

Also, plan to ask Seniors to take on more than one Junior. This works well. Some of our older women have as many as three Heart-to-Heart partners. However, it is important that you not give more than one Senior to a Junior.

In addition, only match women who regularly attend your church. You are not responsible to provide Seniors for young women visiting your Women's Ministries program from other churches.

Question:

What if there are more older women than younger?

Answer:

Rejoice! Begin your program. The younger women of your church and community will be drawn like magnets to your older women. Emphasize the aspect of friendship to your younger women. Some churches have told us that their younger women were hesitant to respond because they mistakenly believed this to be an authoritative relationship.

Question:

How do we encourage our older women to respond? They seem fearful or insecure about their ability to minister to a younger woman.

Answer:

First, ask Seniors in the program to call their friends who are spiritually mature in your church to tell them about the ministry and the need. Second, have Seniors publicly share about their experiences with younger women. Some older women feel intimidated because they think they must be an expert Bible teacher, intellectual genius, or spiritual giant to fill this role. But, when they hear other women share, they can relate and realize how very much they have to offer as well. Emphasize the life experience and friendship aspects of the relationship. Remind them of the value of their life experience.

Question:

What if only a handful of women are truly excited about this ministry?

Answer:

Then start with a handful! As these relationships grow and develop, the joy and satisfaction will be gradually contageous. Continue to teach about the importance of intergenerational friendship.

Question:

What if a Senior signs up who is spiritually immature or emotionally needy? She would simply not be an appropriate role model.

Answer:

First, pray and be kind, loving, and sensitive to her needs. Talk to her, and ask her why she is interested in this program. Many times women will admit they would rather be a Junior, but because of their age, they signed up to be a Senior. Invite them to be Juniors. If this alternative doesn't arise, keep talking. You might find they are extremely busy. Suggest that they wait to avoid overcommitment; they can still minister to younger women through Bible study and church. If they are skilled in another area (choir, administrative) suggest they are truly more needed in that area at present. Ask God to help you find a kind and appropriate reason to suggest their not becoming a Senior. If none of these suggestions works, you may be in a situation where you have to say lovingly, "I think you are dealing with so much in your own life at this time that I believe it would be better to wait. In the meantime, how can we be of help to you?" Or you might tell her that because she is such a new Christian, you believe it would be best for her to wait a couple of years before becoming a Senior. Then suggest great areas of ministry in which she could serve.

111

Question:

What if an extremely needy Junior signs up?

Answer:

Again, pray first, and then talk with her. Explain to her that she needs an older woman's influence and example in her life. But also explain that Heart-to-Heart is not structured to meet the kind of time demand and/or the kind of counseling that she wishes to receive. Tell her you would like to help her find a ministry that would better meet her needs. Lay counseling or professional help might be appropriate. You may find you have an older woman who considers her ministry helping those with deep troubles. Ask your leadership for help if you cannot find an alternative. We have a group of lay women whose skills have been sharpened through courses we offer in our electives. They are available to offer strong, wise support to women who need counsel to change their lifestyle and attitudes and actions or who live in difficult, ongoing situations. Perhaps your pastor would work with you in developing a group such as this in your church.

Question:

How do we avoid problems of gossip?

Answer:

Place continual emphasis on the teaching of Titus 2, not to be malicious gossips. Choose Seniors who have a reputation of confidentiality. Emphasize the responsibility and privilege of confidentiality in speaking with both Juniors and Seniors at various meetings.

Question:

How do we make sure these relationships are strong, close, and growing?

Answer:

You can't! However, you can encourage, pray, and remind the women to keep the relationships close and growing. Moreover, the structure of calls and availability of committee women for input and encouragement does bring a level of accountability. But the relationship is in the hands of the Lord and of the Junior and Senior women who have made their commitments to each other. They are the ones truly responsible for their relationship.

Examples of Forms

Heart-to-Heart Profile Sheet for All Participants

(This sheet should be a full 8½ x 11)

Name _____ Date _____

Address _____ Jr._____ Sr. _____

City _____ Zip _____

Home phone _____ Work phone _____

Age _____ Married _____ Single _____

Best time to be reached by phone: _____

Number and ages of children: _____

Do you attend Women's Ministries? _____ Day _____ Evening

Sunday school class attending _____

How long have you been a Christian? _____

Interests _____

_____

_____

Hobbies _____

_____

_____

Talents _____

_____

_____

Attending the arts _____

Sports _____ Spectator/active _____

Other _____

_____

_____

What I am looking for in a Heart-to-Heart relationship: _____

_____

_____

Please share any other information that would be helpful in making a match.
All women who regularly attend Northwest Bible Church are welcome to participate.

This form should be color-coded using a different color sheet for Jr. and Sr. partners.

Recent Comments

Here are some comments from our most recent set of profile sheets by the Seniors to the question, "What I am looking for in Heart-to-Heart?"

"Friendship and a chance to give back."

"I'd like to find a younger woman to build a friendship with, to love and encourage to walk closely with the Lord, pray with, and have fun with."

"An opportunity to share my experiences (mistakes), strengths, and hopes with someone who wants it."

"Someone to be a big sister to and share my life with."

"Would love to meet someone's needs by sharing how faithful God has been in meeting all my needs in the business world and with three children and a husband."

"Sharing and accountability."

"Someone who needs or wants a friend who doesn't feel 50."

Below are some comments by our Juniors to the same question:

"An older friend who can encourage me, who has been there and can give me wisdom in some frustrating times when I feel life is out of control."

"A Christian friend who knows what it feels like to be a mom at home."

"Someone I can go to for ideas and hints about family life."

"An older, more mature perspective on running a home and raising a family."

"After moving seven times in fifteen years I need someone to share with. My mother died when I was twenty-one so I treasure relationships with older women."

"Someone to confide in."

"Someone who can give me honest, mature, biblical insight and feedback."

"Seeing life from a different perspective—talking to someone who has experienced things I am currently experiencing."

"My mother lives a long way away, and I would like some nurturing, wisdom, and love by an older woman."

"I have no relatives in this area and I often get homesick for my mother's company."

Heart-to-Heart Record Cards

Following is an example of the type of card we keep for follow-up in our Heart-to-Heart program. This aspect of follow-up is particularly important to the ongoing success of the program. Our Heart-to-Heart coordinator and her committee use these cards to keep up with the effectiveness of the matches and to make adjustments when necessary.

```
┌─────────────────────────────────────────────────────────────┐
│                                                             │
│              **Heart-to-Heart Record Cards**                │
│        (for the committee to keep in touch with participants)│
│                                                             │
│   Name _____     │
│   Address _____ Jr. _____ Sr. _____  │
│   City _____ Zip _____   │
│   Home phone _____ Work phone _____     │
│   Age _____ Married _____ Single _____   │
│   Partner assigned _____     │
│   Dates called          Comments                           │
│   _____   _____         │
│                                                             │
│   _____   _____         │
│                                                             │
│   _____   _____         │
│                                                             │
│   _____   _____         │
│                                                             │
└─────────────────────────────────────────────────────────────┘
```

Helpful to use on a 5 x 8 card.
These should be color-coded for Jr. and Sr. partners

Feedback from the Program

Here is some feedback from both Senior and Junior partners who have already participated in Heart-to-Heart.

From the Seniors

"During these days of 'Hi' and 'Bye', it's easy to have many acquaintances, but not so easy to develop friendships. Heart-to-Heart has given me the challenge to really get to know, enjoy, and love some of the younger women in my church; some I probably would never have known."

"As an older woman, I have experienced the joyful and not so joyful times as a wife, mother, and homemaker. I am able to encourage younger women in these areas from a Christian perspective. However, I gain as well as give. I enjoy the concern and love I've received, and I love their youthful vitality, humor, and enthusiasm for life. It keeps me thinking young!"

"I see my Heart-to-Heart role mainly as an encourager. My junior partners are so bright and capable! I just try to help them see their own abilities and worth."

"I love opportunities to share because I always come out knowing more than when I began. The Lord seems to reveal truth in the midst of Heart-to-Heart sharing. Jesus' command to love one another is uppermost in my walk, and I am hungry to form new relationships that go below the surface. I've learned that giving and receiving are never one-sided and that I need the Body. I look forward to being kept up-to-date by a younger person so I don't get out of touch."

"I want to be of help and encouragement to a young mother, to lend a listening and sympathetic ear, to share my experiences that might apply to her situation. I want to show her how God has been faithful and led me through every trial and met every need of my life."

From the Juniors

"I love talking to my senior! She is always nonjudgmental and gives a calm balance to my life. Her strong faith, evident in every situation, is an encouragement. She is a great role model."

"By watching my senior partner demonstrate strength in the midst of tragedy, I learned great lessons about what it means to trust in God, to rest in God, and to know God."

"I have been exceedingly blessed by the spiritual nurturing I have received from my senior partners. One has taught me how to be joyful regardless of circumstances. Another has modeled unselfish giving. My present partner has encouraged me beyond measure to keep time with my Lord and family at the forefront of my life. I so wish to be a godly woman, and I am grateful for their guidance, availability, and loving care."

Easy to Begin

Often the Heart-to-Heart program is a good place to begin your Women's Ministries program. This can form the foundation for a group of women committed to beginning a women's ministry. You can start as small as only two or three matches and grow as the women become increasingly interested. This program also allows the crossover between women who are employed outside the home and those who stay at home.

The following poem was written by one of our young mothers and expresses the needs they feel.

The Women's Ministries
Northwest Bible Church
Heart-to-Heart

Is anyone there
Who would like to share
in my life
as a mother and a wife?
Heart to Heart ...

Could we pray
or talk through my day
share in my joy and sorrow
today and tomorrow?
Heart to Heart ...

Would you give me your view
on what I should do
or lend me your ear
to hear my thought so dear?
Heart to Heart ...

Oh, how I want to live for Jesus
and teach my family how He frees us.
Please show me how to walk in His way
So my life will be full of Him every day
Heart to Heart ...

—Reeve Pearce

PART 4
Cultivating the Garden

The Lord God ... planted a garden.
Genesis 2:8

9
Training and Leadership Development

Relationships

One of the most rewarding aspects of the work on the Women's Ministries program is the development of deep, personal relationships with the women who work closely with me on the board. I believe it is important that the board members be welded together in love and friendship. We encourage this by meeting socially in addition to our regular board meetings.

We have dinner at one member's home every other month with our husbands. The hostess provides the main dish, and each of us brings a dish that completes the meal. This evening together has proven to be beneficial because it gives our husbands exposure to Women's Ministries. When they hear all that we are doing and get to know the women their wives are working with, they are even more supportive of their wives' participation.

We also have a luncheon at Christmas. This is a sweet time of fellowship without having to concentrate on business. We really do have a lot of fun together. When their two years on the board is over, many former members tell me how much they miss that fellowship.

Working Retreats

We select our board replacements for outgoing members by February. Then the new members coming on can work with the person they are replacing to become familiar with their responsibilities. In early May we have an overnight retreat with the current board and the new members. We also invite past board chairmen for their input.

This is a working retreat. Before they come, everyone is asked to revise her job description if it is not accurate. We first take time for prayer and some encouragement from the Bible. Then we review the entire year's program.

As we reflect, we consider such questions as:

> What should we change?
> What should we continue?
> Who would be good for Bible teaching?
> What women can we encourage to serve in some capacity that we have not asked before?

How can we improve our program?
What new areas of outreach should we consider?

We thoroughly discuss everything. We also plan the next year's calendar so that it can be placed on the church calendar as soon as possible.

Accountability

Recently I spoke at a Christmas banquet where they had started a Women's Ministries program along our guidelines. This was their Christmas dinner. Throughout the meal two of the leaders peppered me with questions. "How do you get women to volunteer? How do you get women to take responsibility? What do you do if they don't do their job?"

I found out that the entire dinner, the cooking, and the decorations had fallen almost entirely on these two women. They were discouraged and burned out. I asked if they had committees for these different jobs. Yes, they had. What kind of reports had they had on their progress?

Well, they had asked the various chairmen, "How is the dinner coming?"

"Fine," came back the answer.

However, at the last minute, one chairman became ill, and nothing had been done so it fell to those two women to pick up the slack.

I suggested that in their follow-up they needed much more specific information. They needed to know the names of each person assigned to a specific job. They should have known exactly how much each one had done or their plans to do it at least one month ahead.

Everyone involved in a Women's Ministries activity is accountable to the board, and the board is responsible to supervise every area and help out wherever there is a need. But when someone is not doing her job, she must be confronted lovingly, but firmly. The solution is not to do it for her, as these women did.

Confrontation is something most of us like to avoid. We don't want to hurt someone's feelings. We don't want them to go away mad. We don't want to discourage them from serving. We don't want them to say bad things about us.

But, we must remember, when we are responsible for the spiritual welfare of others we must be diligent to help them develop in various ways. Self-control is one of the areas in which Titus 2 instructs the older women to train the younger women. Helpful and specific follow-up, as well as using people in the area of their giftedness, provides opportunities for success.

Delegation

Sometimes we have to confront a woman because of her way of handling her position. When I see a member of the Women's Ministries Board overburdened with responsibilities, I ask, "Are you delegating?"

Some women will say, "It's easier to do it myself, and it gets done the way that I want it." Then I must remind them that our job as leaders is to give others the opportunity to use their gifts in a protected environment. When there is supervision and accountability, a person is programmed for success rather than failure. Not only that, but we lose the benefits of other women's creativity when we don't let them contribute.

I may have to ask a person who finds it difficult to delegate to give us a list of committee heads within a certain time frame, e.g., two weeks. Delegation develops people, and that is one of our main goals in the women's ministries program.

Team Concept

Sometimes a board position will have varied responsibilities. For instance, the day and evening coordinators must see that the facilities and equipment needed are available and prepared. They must also find someone to lead the music and play the piano. Sometimes another board member is more knowledgeable about the resources for music than the one responsible, so she will offer to take that part of the job.

All of the board is committed to working as a team and helping each member do her job well, sharing the load. There is no place for prima donnas in ministry. We are all servants. Communication helps spread the load when the unexpected occurs.

Nurturing

Part of my role as minister to women is to be available to counsel and encourage the women of the church, especially those in roles of leadership. This means that I take an interest in them and their families and make myself available to them personally and by telephone.

Praise and encouragement must be a large part of your leadership development. I remember a wise woman once told me about my children, "Try to catch them doing something right." The same thought applies to leadership development. Pay close attention to the work of your various board members and try to give them positive feedback on their work.

Another good habit to develop is to pass on positive comments by others to those who have done something especially effective. If we would busy ourselves passing on the positive comments that we hear, we could bury most of the irritating and discouraging negatives.

Nurturing isn't limited to just the board members, however. Our hope is that it is occurring throughout the Women's Ministries program. Women have found that the women's ministry is a safe place, no matter how terrible their past, or how heavy their guilt. Our abortion recovery group has been very successful in bringing about healing in the women who have taken this ten-week course.

I have been asked to speak at a little memorial service the abortion recovery group gives at the end of the series that gives dignity and personal worth to their unborn babies. I always stress that when God forgives sin, He removes it from us, out of reach, out of sight, out of mind, and out of existence. He cleanses our conscience and frees us to serve Him.

Some of these women later give their testimonies before the group to encourage others who have experienced abortion to get help. Each time, several women respond by calling the phone number of the leader. This is all confidential. But I was touched by something I heard recently.

When one of the women gave her testimony recently at Women's Ministries, I just hugged her spontaneously after she was through. Later I heard that one of the other women who eventually took the course said that she did so because of that hug. She said, "I knew it was safe to come."

Evaluation and Feedback

Evaluation and feedback from not only the board members but also from the entire body of women served by the Women's Ministries program is built into our process. We are continually surveying for interest areas and evaluating the effectiveness of the various aspects of the programs.

We are committed to effective ministry and are open to change whenever it seems that we are losing our edge. I also seek feedback from the staff and pastors in my contacts with them.

Innovation

I like to think that we have created an atmosphere open to innovation. Many of our outreach and elective ministries have come when someone has had an idea or burden. If she, or someone else, is willing to head it up, we are open to giving it a try.

There are only a few basic parameters. The ministry must be squarely based on biblical truth, and there must be someone willing to take the responsibility for leading it.

We believe that God is most creative, and we are open to following His direction in our Women's Ministries program.

Accountability in What Is Taught

Another important area of accountability is in what is taught. I heard one of our teachers, who is an avid pet lover, say in answer to a question during one of her lessons that she was sure there would be pets in heaven. She said it with humor, but a Bible teacher has an authority which the Scripture gives and it concerned me.

After praying about it, I made the opportunity to speak to her. First, I praised her for the lesson and all the insights that she had shared. Then I asked her about her statement. What passage in Scripture supported it? I suggested that we have to make a clear distinction between what we wish was true and what we know for certain that the Bible says. She was very gracious, understood what I meant, and thanked me. I felt that I was protecting her ministry as an effective teacher and protecting those who trusted her teaching.

I always listen to tapes of teachers whom I have not personally heard. Once when

I heard the tape of a woman recommended as a retreat speaker, I was mystified by the recommendation. She spent the first fifteen minutes telling jokes like a stand-up comedian. She hardly used any Scripture at all. Her entire message was a potpourri of thoughts about many subjects. It was definitely not the kind of teaching that would build our women spiritually. We must not invite speakers just because they are well known. We must ask: Do they teach God's Word? Do they make it relevant to our lives today?

When we invite a woman to speak for the Bible studies or for our retreats or luncheons, we also ask her to include the gospel. We always assume that there is someone in the audience who doesn't know the Lord. We encourage our women to bring friends and neighbors.

We had a woman who had an important position in Washington speak at our Christmas luncheon recently. She had been told that we wanted her to present the gospel during her message. She gave her own personal testimony about how she had trusted Christ and then continued on to tell us how her unique position stretched her as she trusted the Lord to overcome her fears and enable her to do her job well. Later, when we were eating and I thanked her for giving the gospel so clearly, she told me that she had never done it before as part of her message. She had included it because we asked for it. Now she was very encouraged and said she would make it part of her messages in the future.

Question Time

We have found that a question box placed in the foyer where women can put in questions anonymously is an excellent way to correct misconceptions and help them with personal problems. Sometimes the question will be about something that was taught in the lesson. Either what I said was not clear to them or they got the wrong implication from it.

I am always grateful for an opportunity to correct a misconception or expand on some issue. Sometimes the questions are about other passages that the questioner doesn't understand. The question box protects them from misunderstanding. Sometimes the questions are about personal and family problems. The question box gives the women a way to get some help without embarrassing or incriminating themselves.

Many times a woman will come up later and say, "I was the one who wrote that question." That can give me the opportunity for further counseling.

Unnecessary Offense

When we decided to make aerobics a part of our Women's Ministries program, I was aware that there could be a potential offense from the clothing worn for exercise. Below is a memo from me to all the ladies in aerobics designed to head off unnecessary offense.

We understand that exercising requires different clothing from what one usually wears to church. But since the aerobics electives are an integral part of the Women's Ministries program and we meet on the church campus where men are always walking around, we have a dress code that we ask you to comply with.

If you wear leotards or body suits, please wear loose shorts and a loose top over them. Sweat suits are fine. Just avoid tight or skimpy outfits that are not suitable here. The biblical word for the Christian woman is *modesty!* And that applies even to aerobics. Thanks for your cooperation—and happy aerobics!

Being aware of potential problems and heading them off is usually the better part of wisdom. This principle could apply in many situations.

PART 5

*Gathering a
Bouquet of Flowers*

He produces a crop, yielding a hundred,
sixty or thirty times what was sown.

Matthew 13:23

10
Expected and Experienced Results

Dolores's bright eyes were dancing as she began to share with me how God had led her to accept our invitation to serve on the board as hospitality coordinator. "If anyone had told me four years ago that I would have been able or willing to serve on the Women's Ministries Board, I would have told them they were crazy!"

Her comments didn't really surprise me, but once again I experienced the joy in seeing how God works in the lives of women when they are given an opportunity to grow and develop within the local church in the very way He designed for them.

Dolores had come to the Women's Ministries program as a quiet and retiring woman. She was new in her faith and unsure of any way that she could contribute to the lives of others. Now, only four years later, she was excitedly sharing the outline she had prepared to present from the platform to over two hundred women who were coming to our Women's Ministries Seminar.

Dolores related her excellent ideas about hospitality, how God had answered her specific prayers for such practical things as centerpieces, and how much she had grown in learning to depend on God in all the little details of life.

She had taken one of our elective classes on hospitality in the home. She related how she began to sense that God was drawing her to a greater ministry of hospitality. At first she only thought about it in the context of her home. She made plans to invite various people for meals and was praying about other directions that God would have about hospitality. It was about that time that I called her to ask if she would consider serving on the board position as hospitality coordinator. Her affirmative answer was quick in coming and she joined the board. Her service in that position was so effective that I had asked her to share that job description at the Women's Ministry Seminar.

This blooming of potential spiritual growth is the bouquet of results that I have seen repeated over and over again. Each year I experience the joy of seeing women grow as they exercise their God-given gifts in service to the Body of Christ. This same potential is available through you and the women of your church.

God created women with vast stores of creative talent and energy. They will invest and develop it somewhere. How delightful it is when it can be channeled to the benefit of the work of God through the church. I am thankful for many parachurch organizations that have tapped this creative energy and used it to reach out into our world. They have demonstrated the impact that women can make when they commit their lives to God and His work. However, I am convinced that we need to provide this same opportunity of significant ministry for women within the local church as well.

Here are just a few typical notes I've received about the impact of the Women's Ministries program on the lives of women. You have women just like these in your church.

Dear Vickie,

I consider myself a typical "Dallas Mom" trying to raise small children while striving to grow personally and to be ever fulfilled in order to give my very best to my husband, children, and those around me. Due to the fast pace we live and such a mobile society, I have found raising children can be a *very lonesome* job. Personal fulfillment also seems hard to attain. The Women's Ministries program has more than satisfied three empty areas in my life:

1. Intellectual stimulation
2. Social interaction
3. Small prayer-support groups

Plus I'm happy to be there on Tuesdays! It's a wonderful program that should meet many needs of a large number of busy, happy, but lonesome and/or unfulfilled women here in Dallas.

Dear Vickie,

Thanks for your tireless work in "feeding His sheep." I love Women's Ministries and look forward to learning something new about God every Tuesday. Your efforts are reaching far beyond NBC. As you disciple us, we, in turn, disciple others. I checked out your tape on 1 Corinthians 12 and taught it to a group of ten in my home.

They all expressed how it impacted them. They also have loved learning about spiritual gifts and are convicted to find opportunities to serve the church at large as well as their own local church!

Thanks for making a difference in my life!

As I mentioned earlier, we have available the resource of various types of counselors to assist with problems that surface in the Women's Ministries program. In the context of loving relationships between women, embarrassing and difficult problems are shared. With the structure of support and accountability of the Women's Ministries program, these women can be encouraged, loved, and prayed for. Also, it is often possible to refer them to others who can help in specific areas. The following note is from a single woman who had maxed out on six credit cards. She was over her head and longing for help. We referred her to a couple in our church who counsels those with financial problems. Her life was changed.

Dear Vickie,

Just wanted to thank you for referring me to Don and Suzie. They have been terrific. They are helping me make a spending plan, and it all makes sense, even to me! It's going to be tough, but I feel blessed to have a chance to learn my lesson.

I said earlier that I believe that when women minister to women the entire church is blessed and benefitted. Conversely, the lack of a Women's Ministries program can leave a church without all the warmth and love that women can bring to a congregation. Truly, a church without a vital Women's Ministries program is like a home without a mother. Older women have walked in life where the younger women are walking, and they can make a difference in significant decisions the younger women make and directions they take. God has given us this work for the good of the next generation. We dare not neglect it.

PART 6
An Almanac of Resources

Appendix 1

"Hard Truths About Day Care"

By Karl Zinsmeister

S ome of us have been convinced it is not necessary to actually talk to, cuddle, teach, and comfort our babies ourselves. We parents will just pick out the children's activities, clothes, toys, schedule and diet, while leaving most of the rearing to sitters and housekeepers.

Nearly half of all mothers of preschool children are now employed, and a growing share of America's youngsters are being handed over to hired caretakers. Parents are leaving their children at younger ages, and for longer hours. Child care in large, state-licensed and state-regulated centers is seen by many as the wave of the future.

This mass surrender of child-rearing responsibilities to nonrelatives marks a profound change in human history. While no one has any idea what the ultimate outcome of this giant experiment in proxy child rearing will be, there is growing evidence that the long-term emotional, intellectual, and cultural effects may be unhappy.

"Caution Light"

During the 1970s child psychologist Jay Belsky was one of the first to conclude that day care did not adversely affect child development or give cause for alarm. But then in 1987 he expressed concern over a "slow, steady trickle" of accumulating evidence that contradicted that view. The more recent studies, Belsky pointed out, show two worrisome trends.

First, infants in day care are more likely to develop insecure attachments to their parents. This is so among children in a variety of settings—including day-care centers, homes with a nanny, and family day-care homes. Second, several follow-up studies of children with a record of early nonparental care show more serious aggression, less cooperation, less tolerance of frustration, more misbehavior, and at times, social withdrawal.

Even children with the very best in-home care are at risk. Psychiatrist Peter Barglow and colleagues at Michael Reese Hospital in Chicago examined 110 one-year-olds from affluent families. Half were cared for full time by a parent; half had stable, hired caretakers. The substitute-care infants turned out to have significantly less-secure relationships with their mothers. The researchers concluded that many infants interpret daily separations from their working mothers as rejection, with which they cope by withdrawing from her. This finding corroborated another study of middle-class children in Michigan. It found that one-year-olds in full-time day care displayed greater avoidance of their mothers than did parent-reared infants.

Another study of five- to eight-year-olds who had spent most of their first years at a highly regarded day-care center at the University of North Carolina discovered they were more likely to hit, kick, threaten, and argue than those not in day care or who started later. Research involving middle-class children in the Dallas area found that those who spent extensive time in day care were more uncooperative, less popular, and had poorer grades and study skills, and less self-esteem by third grade.

Controversy rages, and it appears that factors such as a child's temperament, family status and economic background, as well as the quality of the program, have a lot to do with how the youngster adapts to day care. Also, risks associated with full-time day care sometimes disappear when the care is just part-time. Age seems to be critical. What might be disorienting for a toddler can often be handled adequately by an older preschooler. Clearly, though, the findings of the last few years should signal a "caution light" and give us reason to hesitate in our uncritical plunge toward more child raising by hire.

Damage Reports

Even before this latest evidence started coming in, many leading child-development experts discouraged day care's early use. If you took your cues only from the glowing endorsements of day care by the activists and the "children's defense" groups, you might never have learned that many pediatricians, child psychologists, and educational theorists have long argued that any significant amount of nonparental care is unhealthy for very young children.

Penelope Leach, the British psychologist and author of perhaps the most influencial child-raising handbook in America, *Your Baby and Child*, is a leading opponent of the trend toward mothers having to go to work and leave their small children. She insists that babies need individual care for at least two years.

Burton White, author of *A Parent's Guide to the First Three Years* and former director of the Harvard Preschool Project, says, "After more than 30 years of research on how children develop well, I would not think of putting an infant or toddler of my own into any substitute-care program on a full-time basis, especially a center-based program. Unless you have a very good reason, I urge you not to delegate the primary child-rearing task to anyone else during your child's first three years of life. Babies form their first human attachment only once."

Child pyschoanalyst Selma Fraiberg says that regular absences by the mother can be damaging for children under three. Only from ages three to six, she states, can most children profit from a half-day in high-quality group care. But even then, she writes, "there is a consensus among preschool educators that the benefits of a good preschool program diminish or are even canceled when the school day is prolonged to six hours or beyond."

Child's-Eye View

The medical establishment, too, has voiced reservations about day care. The American Medical Association warned in 1983 that day-care centers—where drooling, diapered, toy-sucking infants put their fingers in their mouths an average of every three minutes—were becoming dangerous sources of infections. According to the Centers for Disease Control and other authorities, day-care centers are responsible for rising levels of diarrhea, dysentery, giardiasis, epidemic jaundice, hepatitis A, ear and cytomegalovirus (CMV) infections.

The critical factor in judging day care is point of view. If you are looking at it from the point of view of economically and socially ambitious parents, day care is clearly a great convenience. But in the rush to simplify and cushion the lives of adults, it is easy to overlook the interests of the children involved. Indeed, I have been amazed as I've followed the day-care debate to see how infrequently it is approached with a child's eye view. It is argued as a "women's issue," as an "employment issue," as a "productivity issue"; but scarcely anyone asks, "Is it good for children?"

A common response to the rising negative evidence on day care is to say that it is insensitive and unfair to burden parents with such reports. As one activist puts it, "Telling them that they're endangering their child's future emotional well-being is a disservice; it just adds to the guilt and anxiety they already feel." Of course, she is right that this is horribly inconvenient news. But parents want the facts, not a lulling from apologists.

Tedium and Tears

For her book *A Mother's Work,* Deborah Fallows spent hundreds of hours in dozens of centers in Massachusetts, Texas, Maryland, and Washington, D.C. While Fallows discovered no abuse, little dirt, and adequate physical conditions in most centers, she found the average child's experience to be frighteningly empty.

A day-care center has a continual "on" atmosphere, which leaves little time for children to muse, and where the pressure of numbers pushes even gentle and reserved children to react constantly. Grace saying, coat donning, one-at-a-time hand washing—these become exhausting trials in depersonalization.

Fallows gives wrenching descriptions of children referred to as "hey, little girl" and of activities that cater to the group average but leave quiet children behind. She tells of desperate notes sent in by parents pleading for extra attention and special comfort. There is much tedium, much bewilderment, many unconsoled tears. Children wandering about, constantly clamoring to go "to Mommy's house," are quieted with fibs ("Mommy will be here soon").

While day care provided in homes tends to be less impersonal than the center-based variety, it also has many problems. For one, there will never be enough individuals willing to take care of other people's children. And although home-based care has the potential to be healthiest for children, it also invites the most dangerous abuses, such as those we often read about in newspapers.

Writer and mother Linda Burton encountered some of these common problems when she began searching for home-based day care: "On one unannounced visit, I found that the 'highly recommended' licensed day-care provider confined seven preschoolers to her tiny dining room. They were huddled together, leaning over a barricade, watching a TV in the next room."

Even the gold standard of day care—a nanny-type arrangement in the child's own home—has serious problems. The most common is frequent turnover of care-givers, which can be emotionally disruptive for the child.

Basically, it appears that whether the day care takes place in a center, a private house or at the child's home, similar risks result. The question is: can you substitute a paid relationship for the natural parent-child bond without seriously harming children and society? It appears the answer may be no.

What Can We Do?

At present, all of the aggressive efforts of the increasingly powerful day-care lobby head in the wrong direction. Day-care activists insist that helping parents stay at home when their children are very young is absurd, since working parents are a "reality." Advocates implicitly discourage the form of day care least likely to be harmful—informal care in a relative's or friend's house—on the ground that it is not standardized and regulated, not professional enough.

The fundamental push of day-care advocacy today is away from the personal and the small, and toward big, regulated "young age homes" run by professional baby-sitters.

Of course these centers are the places least likely to give children what they need. But all existing bonuses, options, and subsidies push in their direction. For instance, our current child-care tax credit, which funnels about $4 billion annually to parents, can be claimed only by people who pay others to provide the care. It cannot be claimed by parental care givers. The proposed ABC bill now before Congress would allow funds to go only to state-sanctioned centers, bypassing informal caretakers such as relatives and friends, and probably church-based groups as well, for First Amendment reasons.

Rather than further subsidizing substitute parenting, with its many risks, we ought to endeavor to create options for the large number of Americans who would like to care for their own children when they are very young. There is much we can do in this area, from enacting tax credits for parents raising preschoolers, to encouraging more home-based work, to changing social attitudes about the contributions of stay-at-home parents.

Supporters of mass day-care outside the home contend it is helpful in teaching children to "socialize," and point to its importance in early learning. Day-care children, to be sure, often start out ahead of their home-raised peers in things like knowing the alphabet when they begin kindergarten. But does this amount to anything? Kids under age four, authorities tell us, should not be praised for academic achievement. Little more than creative play ought to be expected from them.

What the very young want, and urgently need, child-development experts agree, is not education or socialization, but the affection and unhurried attention of their parents. (And fathers as much as mothers ought to take responsibility for the upbringing of their children.)

A majority of day-care workers are conscientious and try to substitute for the missing parents, but fail for a number of reasons. One problem is sheer numbers—a single caretaker typically looks after four to 15 children, depending on their age and the setting. Another is continuity. Child developmentalists tell us that rapid shuffling of guardians is extremely traumatizing to a small child.

But the deepest problem with paid child-rearing is that someone is being asked to do for money what very few of us are able to do for any reason other than love. Competent and safe baby-sitters are not hard to hire. What will always be difficult is finding people who feel such affinity with the child that they will go out of their way to do the tiny, precious things that make children thrive—giving a reason why rather than just saying no, rewarding a small triumph with a joyful expression, showering unqualified devotion.

The truth is, a day-care worker is doing a job. If he or she manages simply to be a kind friend to the youngster and a reliable guardian of the child's safety, that is all anyone ought to expect. Giving the child the rest of what he needs—a self-image, a moral standard, life ambitions, and a sense of permanent love—is too much to ask of anyone other than the parents.

Appendix 2

A Report to the Governing Body of a Local Church

*B*elow is an outline of the initial report presented to the elders of Northwest Bible Church to enlist their support. The women prepared and duplicated the report, and a copy was presented to each elder at a special dinner hosted by the committee.

Page 1   The cover sheet was an attractive pink. We used the logo for the Women's Ministries program that one of our women designed. You could develop your own, or simply use the title "Women's Ministries."

Page 2   On this page we summarized the result of the survey of our women. We included a statement of the needs, several points about our proposal, and the points of action being requested.

Page 3   This page listed the names of the women on the working committee, as well as a list of the various women who had served in an advisory capacity.

Page 4   This page carried an organizational chart showing the various aspects of the Women's Ministries program and how they related to one another. This page is included in this Appendix as it shows how existing ministries were included in the overall transition plan.

Page 5   This page listed the "Proposed Schedule for the Weekly Program," as well as the anticipated dates for sessions in the upcoming year.

Page 6   This page listed the Bible teachers planned for the upcoming sessions, as well as a list of the various kinds of electives, together with their leaders.

Page 7   This page carried a job description for the requested position of director of Women's Ministries, including qualifications and responsibilities.

Page 8   This page was for a letter from the pastor to the elders indicating his support of the program as proposed by the committee.

Page 9   The final pages contained quotes from well-known people and from some of our own women about the importance of a Women's Ministries program. I have included those quotations in this workbook.

Page 10   This page was a matching cover sheet in attractive pink.

Organizational Chart for a Women's Ministries Program

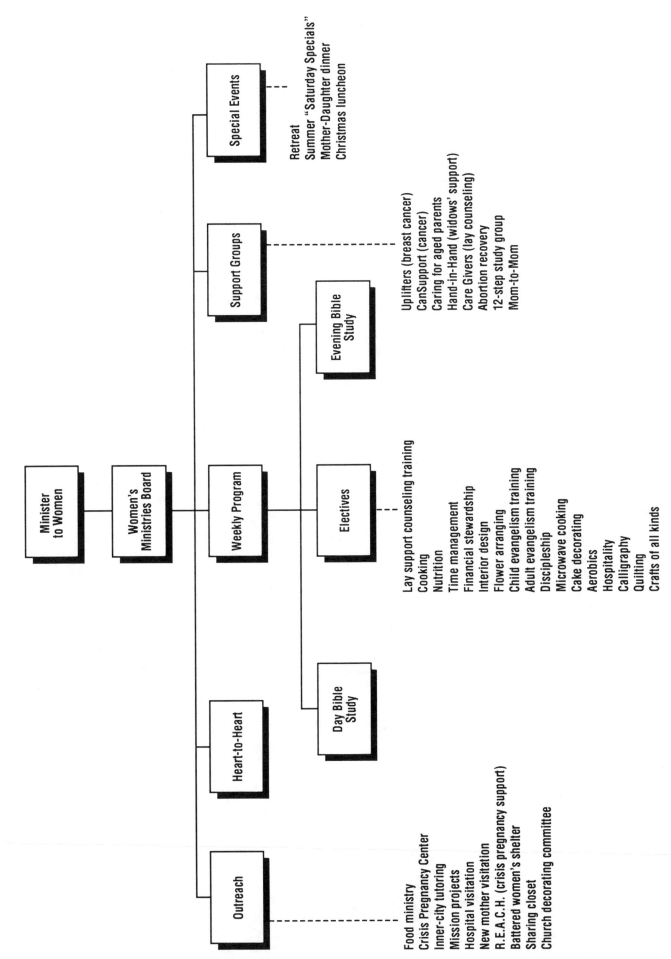

Minister to Women

Women's Ministries Board

Outreach

Food ministry
Crisis Pregnancy Center
Inner-city tutoring
Mission projects
Hospital visitation
New mother visitation
R.E.A.C.H. (crisis pregnancy support)
Battered women's shelter
Sharing closet
Church decorating committee

Heart-to-Heart

Weekly Program

Day Bible Study

Electives

Lay support counseling training
Cooking
Nutrition
Time management
Financial stewardship
Interior design
Flower arranging
Child evangelism training
Adult evangelism training
Discipleship
Microwave cooking
Cake decorating
Aerobics
Hospitality
Calligraphy
Quilting
Crafts of all kinds

Evening Bible Study

Support Groups

Uplifters (breast cancer)
CanSupport (cancer)
Caring for aged parents
Hand-in-Hand (widows' support)
Care Givers (lay counseling)
Abortion recovery
12-step study group
Mom-to-Mom

Special Events

Retreat
Summer "Saturday Specials"
Mother-Daughter dinner
Christmas luncheon

In Support of Change . . .

"There has been a dynamic change in women's lives. . . . Their time scheduling is very important, so just a Bible study format is not enough. Women's groups are struggling all over the country. We need to be much more diverse to meet everyone's needs. . . . No one needs just another meeting."

Jeanne Hendricks

"I agree wholeheartedly that it was wise for you to discontinue the old format for a year. I haven't seen that format work well for a long time. It takes something *specialized* to make women come to something apart from their husbands."

Anne Ortland

"A century ago, women cooked together, canned together, washed clothes at the creek together, prayed together. . . . Alas, the situation is very different today. The extended family has disappeared, depriving the wife of that source of security and fellowship. . . . The difference between them can be seen in the breakdown in relationship between women! Instead, you must achieve a network of women friends with whom you can talk, laugh, gripe, dream, and recreate."

Dr. James Dobson, *Straight Talk to Men and Their Wives*

"Stuart Briscoe stated in an article in *Moody Monthly* in February 1983 entitled, 'The Biblical Woman, We've Buried a Treasure': 'We know the Holy Spirit gifts all believers, including women, for the upbuilding of the church and the glory of God.

'The Master has great numbers of female servants. . . . They seem to have a great heart for the Lord; they love to study the Word of God and are eager to pray.

'But even though they are so numerous and so interested, the full force of cumulated talents doesn't seem to have been released. So great has been the burial that some of us think the greatest wasted resource in the chruch is women-power. . . . A talent is a terrible thing to waste.' "

From *Northwest Women*

D. T. expressed concern for lack of unity within the body. She stated that she has never felt that she and her husband were an integral part of Northwest, and had even attended other churches, but had always come back because of the teaching. She expressed excitement about the proposed plan because it offered a solution.

"If the women of the church were united, there's no end as to what might happen."

G. D., from Northwest Bible Church

Appendix 3

Women's Ministries Tapes and a Sample of Study Questions

Women's Ministries Tapes

Bible lessons by Vickie Kraft.

God's Power for Our Inadequacy: The Life of Moses (24 lessons)

Timeless Solutions to 20th Century Problems: A Study of 1 Corinthians (23 lessons)

Character Study: Joseph, Product of a Dysfunctional Family (8 lessons)

Jesus Christ: God Revealed (9 lessons)
      Jesus Christ: God Revealed
      Miracle at Cana
      The Samaritan Woman
      Widow at Nain
      Invitation to Dinner
      Feeding the Hungry
      Light of the World
      Healing on the Sabbath
      Widow's Offering

God's Women (8 lessons)
      God's Woman (Proverbs 31)
      Miriam
      Why Do Bad Things Happen to Good People? (Widow and Oil)
      Bait for the Trap, Women Caught in Adultery
      Jesus Heals Two Women (Mark 5:22-43)
      Priscilla and Aquila
      Lydia: Homemaker, Business Woman (Acts 16)
      Mary Magdalene, Significant Single

Born Free! (A Study of Galatians) (8 lessons)
      Born Free from the World System
      Born Free from Requirements of the Law
      Born Free from the Penalty of the Law
      Born Free from the Power of Sin

Born Free from the Slavery of Sin
Born Free to Stand Firm in Christ's Freedom
Born Free from the Sinful Nature
Born Free to Be Ourselves and Serve Others

Winning God's Approval: A Study of the Characters in Hebrews 11 (10 lessons)
Overview of Hebrews
Cain and Abel
Noah, Majority of One
Abraham and Sarah
Moses
Joshua
Rahab
Daniel
Deborah
Keep on Running

Philippians (7 lessons)

Colossians (8 lessons)

Individual tapes may be purchased by mail for $5.00 for each by mailing a check to:
Titus 2:4 Ministries
P.O. Box 797566
Dallas, TX 75379-7566

Hebrews 11:4

Vickie Kraft

Questions—Lesson 2

1. Read the book of Hebrews through this week. Underline key words such as: *better, blood, faith, High Priest, eternal, let us,* and *Son.*
2. Read Genesis 4. In what ways were Cain and Abel the same? In what ways were they different?
3. How did their worship differ?
4. List Cain's downward progression.
5. Why did he kill Abel? (Matthew 23:35; 1 John 3:12).
6. Was Cain a believer who sinned, or an unbeliever? (1 John 3:12).
7. What evidence is there that Cain belonged to the evil one? (John 8:44).
8. Count how many times the word *brother* is used in Genesis 4 and in 1 John 3:12. Why do you think this is emphasized?
9. What do we learn of the character of God in His dealings with Cain?
10. What two basic approaches to God do the two offerings present?

Digging Deeper

1. What is implied by the statement in Hebrews 11 that "by faith Abel offered a better sacrifice"? What is necessary for faith? (Romans 10:17). Suggest the significance of Genesis 3:24 in this regard.
2. What did the offering of animals teach the offerer about God, man, sin, and salvation?
3. What did the blood of Abel speak out for? (Hebrews 12:24). What is the "better word" of which the blood of Christ speaks? (1 John 1:7; John 1:29, Hebrews 9:12, 14, 22; 10:19).
4. What is the significance of the first man born murdering the second in the light of Romans 5:12-21?
5. How would you describe the "way of Cain"? (Jude 11).

Application Questions

1. What does 1 John 3:12 tell us about the attitude of unbelievers toward believers? Why is it important to understand this basic fact to have a proper worldview? Does this passage help you to understand a difficult relationship you may be experiencing now?
2. What are some of the reasons we can begin to hate other believers? If we have a "just" cause and the one who harmed us gives no sign of repentance or desire for forgiveness, are we justified in harboring resentment?
   a. What must we do? (Matthew 18:15-17; Ephesians 4:32).
   b. Why is it necessary? (Hebrews 12:14).
   c. Who gets the advantage when we don't forgive?
   d. Is there someone in your life now that you are bitter toward? What will you do about it on the basis of this lesson?
   e. If the situation doesn't change, how can you change? (1 Thessalonians 5:1-8, 4:1; Philippians 4:8).
   f. How can forgiving be done by faith?
3. How does a person today attain a right relationship with God? What works

does she have to do? How can anyone know that she will continue in that relationship? What does one have to do to stay there? (Ephesians 2:8-10; John 10:27-29; John 6:28, 29; John 5:24).

Hebrews 11:30-31
Vickie Kraft

Questions—Lesson 6

1. Why was God giving Israel the land of Canaan? (Genesis 12:1; 15:12-20; 28:13-15; Exodus 3:7-8, 16-17).
2. What did God want to teach these people by doing this? Remember, they had lived for 400 years in a nation that was grossly idolatrous. (Deuteronomy 4:32-40; esp. 36-38).
3. What did the king's orders in Joshua 2:2 indicate about the knowledge of the people of Jericho concerning Israel and her future? See also Joshua 9:9-11, 24.
4. What was the state of the morale in Jericho? (Joshua 2:9, 11; 6:1). How does this confirm God's promises in Deuteronomy 1:21, 29, 31?
5. Read carefully Joshua 2:9-13. What did Rahab know about Israel's history? How long before had the Red Sea been crossed? (Exodus 14; Deuteronomy 2:7). How long before had Sihon and Og been conquered? (Deuteronomy 2:26—3:11).
6. What did Rahab specifically say she believed about the God of Israel? What is impressive about her fatih? Could anyone else in Jericho have come to the same conclusions?
7. How did she demonstrate her faith? What risk was she taking? (Joshua 2:4-7, 12-13, 21; James 2:25).
8. How was her faith rewarded? (Joshua 2:12-13, 27-21; 6:22-24; Matthew 1:5).
9. What conclusions do you draw from Rahab's inclusion in the genealogy of Jesus Christ? (Matthew 1:5). How did Jesus treat immoral women when He was here on earth? (John 4; John 8:1-11).

Digging Deeper

1. How do you reconcile Rahab's disobeying and lying to her king when compared to the principle stated in Romans 13:1-6? See also 2 Samuel 19:11-17; Exodus 1:15-20; Acts 4:19; 5:29.
2. Note the word used to describe the rest of the people of Jericho, *disobedient.* What were they disobedient regarding? (Romans 1:18-32; 2:14-15). For the same concept see Ephesians 2:2; 5:6, 12; Titus 3:3; and Romans 1:5.
3. What happened between the episode of the spies and the conquest of Jericho? (Joshua 3). With this knowledge, when the people of Jericho saw the army marching around their walls for seven days, what could they have done? (Joshua 2:9-14). See also 9:9-11, 24.
4. What does the mention of this woman three times in the New Testament tell us about the grace of God and the nature of sin? Study Romans 3:9-26 and list.

Application Questions

1. Do you feel that some sins in your past or present are so terrible that they

can't be forgiven, or that you are unworthy to serve God? How does the story of Rahab encourage you? Read Colossians 3:1-17 to see how God views you and your responsibilities as His child. Memorize Colossians 3:1-4.

2. Acts 26:17-18 and 1 Thessalonians 1:9 reveal that a drastic change took place in the lives of these early believers, as it did with Rahab. Has your life changed substantially since you trusted Christ, or do you have a foot in both worlds? What do you need to stop? To start doing?

3. Notice how the total person was involved in Rahab's faith: her mind had facts (Joshua 2:8-11), her emotions reacted (2:11), her will made a decision, and she acted (2:12-14). This is always involved in true faith. It's not enough to know about Jesus Christ, but with an act of our will we must personally trust Him as Savior. Have you done this? This also applies to the process of growth as a Christian—the will must decide and act.

Galatians 4:1-31

Vickie Kraft

Questions—Lesson 5

1. (Vv. 1-7) What would be the differences in the positions, privileges, and responsibilities between a mature son and heir, and a slave in a household?

2. (V. 7) God has made us His heirs. Study the following passages to get some insight about this inheritance: Romans 8:16, 17; Ephesians 3:6-12; Hebrews 1:2; 1 Peter 1:3-6; 3:7. Do you actually think of yourself as God's heir? How would that change your view towards life and goals here on earth?

3. (V. 4) What is the purpose of Christ's redemption here? Compare with 1:4, 3:14. What does this verse and the following passages (John 1:15; 3:16; 1 John 4:14; and Hebrews 2:24) tell us about Jesus' humanity and its purpose?

4. (Vv. 8-10) What were the Galatians and all Gentiles formerly slaves to? (1 Corinthians 12:2, 10:19, 20). By placing themselves under the law for sanctification, what were they in danger of being enslaved to now?

5. (Vv. 12-20) Paul was like a father in the way he treated the Galatians. What principles for discipling children can we learn from this section?

6. (V. 16) This verse reveals the risk we face when we confront someone with the truth. Has this ever happened to you? What did you do as a result?

7. (Vv. 17-18) What were the motives of the false teachers?

8. (V. 19) What was Paul's goal for his ministry? What should be your goal for yourself and other believers? (Romans 8:29; Ephesians 4:13-15; Colossians 1:27). How can you accomplish this?

9. (Vv. 21-31) Read Genesis 16:1-16 and 21:1-21 for background. What words are used to describe Hagar and Sarah? (22, 23, 30, 31). What does each represent? (24).

10. (V. 29) What is always the attitude of legalism towards grace?

11. (Vv. 30-31) What is Paul saying about law and grace, works and faith, and bondage and freedom here?

12. (Vv. 28-31) Whose child are you?

13. Since you were born *free*, what impact should that make on your concept of living to please God and growing to maturity? (1 Thessalonians 4:1). How

can you achieve this goal? (Romans 6:6-18). What is God's part? What is your part?

14. Can you think of a sin you are enslaved to? Take the steps in Romans 6:11-14 and trust the Spirit of God to set you free in this specific area.

Why Do Bad Things Happen to Good People? Vickie Kraft

Questions—2 Kings 4:1-7

1. What was the spiritual condition of the northern kingdom, Israel, as exemplified by her kings? (2 Kings 1:1-3; 3:1-3).
2. What do we know about the widow's husband from verse 1? Write down all you can deduce from these brief statements.
3. What do you learn about the "company (or sons) of the prophets"? Who were they? What did they do? Who were their leaders? (See 1 Kings 20:35; 2 Kings 2:3, 5, 7, 15; 4:1, 38; 5:22; 6:1; 9:1.)
4. The Mosaic law provided for paying off debts by working (Leviticus 25:39-41). How did God limit this practice?
5. What responsibility did God place on the entire community regarding widows and orphans? (Exodus 22:22, 23; Deuteronomy 14:28; 24:19-21). Did Israel obey God in this? (Isaiah 1:17, 23; 10:1).
6. What does God promise to do? (Deuteronomy 10:18; Psalm 68:5).
7. Why did the widow come to Elisha? What was especially pathetic about her situation?
8. What does Elisha's response tell us about him? (2 Kings 4:2a).
9. What do you deduce from the fact that he used what she had as a resource? Compare Exodus 4:1-5; Mark 6:35-44. Write down a principle that you can derive from this. Can you now make a specific application of this principle to your own life?
10. List all the things that Elisha commanded her to do. Why did he have her ask her neighbors for jars?
11. What impact do you think this incident had on her sons? In what practical ways can you show your children what God is like?
12. What had she asked Elisha's help for? What did she actually receive?
13. How did this destitute widow become an influence in her day? In our day?
14. How did God "defend her cause"? (Deuteronomy 10:18). Compare 1 Kings 17:1-24 and note the similarities.
15. What is our responsibility today to the orphan and widow? (1 Timothy 1:16; James 1:27). What do they need besides material provisions? Is there someone you can provide any of this for *this week*?
16. What does God expect of us as women in our homes, church, and community? (Romans 12:1-21; Galatians 6:9-10). Study these passages and ask God to reveal a specific area where He wants you to be obedient to Him as you reach out to meet someone's need.

Appendix 4

Instructions for Support Groups and Outreach Ministries

Uplifters

Uplifters is a support ministry through which women who have had breast cancer support breast cancer patients and their families. We are available to ladies who have discovered a breast lump and need to talk. We answer questions pertaining to breast cancer and breast disease. An Uplifter will talk with anyone from our church as well as the community. We meet only as needed. On occasion, Uplifters will eat lunch together. At this time, we support each other through our friendships and our prayers. This is a very special group to each of us who are directly involved. Anyone who has had breast cancer and who desires to serve others is welcome to join.

Areas of outreach are:

1. One-on-one support ministry—described above.
2. CanSupport—a cancer support group for women who have experienced cancer. This group is open to ladies from our church and our community. CanSupport meets monthly on the second Tuesday during lunch at 12:15 P.M. till everyone leaves. The ladies bring a sack lunch to eat, talk, and pray for each other and others who are unable to attend. CanSupport chose to meet during the lunch hour so that those who work can attend.
3. Yearly Screening Mammography—A local hospital-based mammography mobile unit comes to campus at Northwest Bible Church during our Women's Ministries Tuesday morning and Wednesday night sessions. Mammograms done through this mobile unit cost less than through a private physician and are more convenient.
4. Caring and Sharing, Women-to-Woman—Uplifter offered this class during the Tuesday morning Women's Ministries electives a year ago. Our purpose was to learn appropriate sharing and caring techniques for difficult circumstances. These biblically based principles were taught by women who have experienced various difficulties. Some of the subjects discussed were coping with elderly parents, helping the chronically ill person, and the death of a loved one.
5. Uplifters will assist any church starting its own group. Please ask us.

Resources for Uplifters

Pamphlets:
Mom Is Very Sick—Here's How to Help, by Wendy Bergren

My Child Is Very Sick—Here's How to Help, by Sissy Gaes
Order from Focus on the Family, 4010 North Cascade Ave., Colorado Springs, CO 80903.
Paperback books:
When the Doctor Says It's Cancer, by Mary Beth Moster. Available from local bookstores or Tyndale House Publishers.
God's Faithfulness in Trials and Testings, by Sandy Edmonson. Order from Missionary Crusader International, 2451 34th St., Lubbock, TX 79511-1689.
Then the Sun Came Up, by Helen Palston Tucker. Star Books, Inc., 408 Pearson St., Wilson, NC 27893.
My Book for Kids with Cancer, by Jason Gaes. Melius and Peterson Publishing, Inc., 524 Citizens Bldg., Aberdeen, SD 57401
Cassette
Surviving Breast Cancer, Dr. James Dobson and panel. Focus on the Family, 4010 North Cascade Ave., Colorado Springs, CO 80903.

R.E.A.C.H.

Primary Goal

To direct the life of a client toward the goal of becoming a functional family unit (married, single, or birth mother) founded on the love and forgiveness of Jesus Christ.

Volunteer Requirements

A believer in Jesus Christ who accepted the love and forgiveness of a risen Savior and is called into this work to share with a client the love and forgiveness she has received.

Client Requirements

Any client with a positive pregnancy test who recognizes the need for help and support and is willing to become acqainted with and work with a Support Volunteer. Some clients are referred to us from the Crisis Pregnancy Center.

Goals of Support Volunteer

I. Meeting the spiritual needs of the client
   A. Spiritual example
   B. Pray to lead client to the Lord
   C. Help client to grow in the Lord
   D. Attempt to plug client into a church body
   E. Help client to understand the biblical view of sex
   F. Have a prayer warrior praying daily for client

II. Help client to set goals
   A. Examine and work through the options of marriage, single parenting, and adoption
   B. Encourage client to attend parenting classes given by CPC and discuss successful parenting skills

C. Work through plans for after the baby—school, work, living accommodations, child care needs, and so on

III. Physical needs
    A. Access needs and research church, CPC, and community for help
    B. Baby shower
    C. Food taken over after the birth of the baby
    D. Provide transportation when possible to doctor, and so on

How to Start a R.E.A.C.H. Ministry in Your Church

1. Seek counsel, approval, and prayer support of your pastor and elder board.
2. Find some key people who have a heart for helping women and who would be willing to spearhead the new ministry for young girls who choose life for their babies in the midst of a crisis pregnancy. You need a group of mature, committed women who will stick in there when it seems like things are at a standstill or there is a ton of work to be done. Many of these people end up being your leadership. Although they may still be involved with individual clients and may be support volunteers themselves, they mainly serve as security and protection for the other volunteers. They essentially keep the ministry going, i.e., undergird with prayer, keep everyone together, problem-solve, and pour out the emotional support to the other volunteers, especially those who have a client.
3. Get the leadership core (if possible include some of the church leaders) together to decide what you will and will not do. Come up with your own guidelines, strategies, and plans to recruit other volunteers.
4. Establish a "pipeline" of women in need. Once you have this core in place you need to decide where your prospective clients will come from, i.e., CPC, your own church, sidewalk counseling, other pro-life groups. There are plenty of women out there, but we have sometimes found it hard to find them. Lack of clients is worse than lack of volunteers because you need to keep your volunteers motivated and excited and give them something to do or they will lose interest.
5. Take on your first client and see how the guidelines, strategies, and plans work. These will evolve as you run into different clients with different needs and situations.
6. Recruit others to help and also pray. Seek to use people with different gifts and talents. Get the word out through Sunday school classes, the church bulletin, women's Bible studies, and so on.

Healing the Hurts of Abortion

Considering that millions of babies have been aborted since abortion was legalized in the United States, there are many women and men within our churches who have been hurt by abortion. The purpose of our ministry is to become a "Good Samaritan" to those hurting. Through a ten-week Bible study we help them recognize how God sees abortion and recognize their need to confess their part in the abortion(s). We then show them through the Bible God's grace and forgiveness and that God forgives them, and that they need to forgive themselves and others.

We allow these victims of abortion to give their baby(ies) identity and dignity and to grieve the loss of their babies. Throughout our class, we provide love, prayer, support, and encouragement. Each person attending our class has her own "care taker" who ministers to her individual needs.

We use the curriculum "Healing the Hurts of Abortion," written by Ken Freeman of Last Harvest Ministries, a pro-life ministry here in Dallas. We announce our class at Women's Ministries, in the adult Sunday school classes, and in the church bulletin. Also, Ken Freeman refers women to us who have called his hot-line number requesting help in dealing with the hurts of their abortion(s).

It is wonderful to see women returning to the Lord as this Bible study presents God's truths and surrounds the people we are ministering to with God's love.

Mom-to-Mom

Goals and Objectives:

Goal: To encourage mothers of young children

Objectives: Information/Program
                      Practical
                      Spiritual
          Prayer and Sharing
          Outreach/Publicity
          Fellowship/Friendship
          Internal Communications/Prayer Chain
          Nursery
          Food
          Service to Others

Program Chairman and Coordinator of Steering Committee

Plan stimulating programs, spiritual and practical

Set up room, coordinate with the scheduling secretary and the church calendar

Turn in room arrangement

Introduce the speaker

Program time—10:00-11:00

Plan transition into prayer time with prayer and sharing leader

Write thank-you note to speaker

Prayer and Sharing

Begins at 11:00

Promote informal, nonthreatening prayer and sharing

Plan "creative" ways for entire group to share in an effective and nurturing manner

Hostess

Be available to greet members and guests at 9:15

Permanent name tags and signs

Assist with attendance records and membership roster updates
    Follow-up
    Coordinate with prayer chain leaders

Plan informal fellowship and introduction from 9:15-10:00

Begin program at 10:00 sharp!! with program chairman

Plan informal function once a year for spouses

Function as contact person for new members and visitors

Secretary

Liaison with hostess to update membership rosters
    Mail: Calendar
            Program Plans
            Membership Roster
            Prayer Chain

Internal communications among committee members

Maintain membership roster

Have calendar, membership roster, and prayer chains available at the meetings

Contact Coordinator

Organize prayer chain
Coordinate prayer chain leaders
    Duties: Monthly nursery and lunch count
        Maintain contact with group
        Follow up absences, illnesses, needs
Activate the prayer chain as the need arises
Keep contact group roster current, add and delete names as needed
Inform membership of the functions of the prayer chain

Outreach/Publicity

Liaison with Women's Ministries Board
Purpose is to inform church body of our ministry
Update announcements and information in church bulletin, church calendar,
    church newsletter, and Women's Ministries brochures
Keep informed of upcoming programs and changes
Coordinate with program director and secretary

Nursery

Liaison with contact group leaders
Liaison with church nursery staff for:
    number of nursery workers needed
    number of actual reservations
    exact dates and times of meetings for the year
Nursery coordinator's name and phone number must be on all publications
    Nursery reservations are to be stressed
Encourage participation in Women's Ministries

Food

Organize luncheons on Tuesdays (3) and one picnic
Organize brunches on Wednesdays with prayer chain leaders
Delegate luncheon preparations to group members
Set up food service area
Supervise cleanup of food service and meeting areas

Service

Dallas Life Foundation—coordinate cake, cupcakes, and drink for birthday party
    one day a month
Visitation to New Mothers:
    Coordinate with outreach/publicity in supplying visitation committee with
        information about our meetings
    Coordinate with hostess and secretary about new mothers who may be visit-
        ing our group
    Coordinate new mother visitation within moms' group
    Assist coordinator of new mother visitation ministry in keeping a current list
        of pregnant ladies/due date roster

Suggested Reading List for Twelve-Step Groups

The Big Book, Alcoholics Anonymous

One Day at a Time in Al-Anon, Al-Anon Family Group Headquarters

Recovery: A Guide for Adult Children of Alcoholics, Hebert L. Gravitz and Julie D. Bowden, Fireside (Simon & Schuster Trade)

Adult Children of Alcoholics, Janet G. Woitiz, Health Comm.; also G. K. Hall (large print)

Codependent No More, Melody Beattie, Hazelden; also Harper Collins; also Walker (large type)

Beyond Codependency, Melody Beattie, Harper Collins

Peoples' Pharmacy, rev. ed., Joe Graedon, St. Martins

Women Who Love Too Much, Robin Norwood, Pocket; also Tarcher (hardback; distrib. by St. Martins)

Permission to Be Precious, Pia Mellody (tapes)

Struggle for Intimacy, Janet Woitiz, Health Comm.

The Dance of Anger, Harriet Goldhor Lerner, Harper Collins

After the Tears, Jane Middleton-Moz and Lorie Dwinell, Health Comm.

Grandchildren of Alcoholics, Ann Smith, Health Comm.

Inside Out, Larry Crabb, NavPress

Healing for Damaged Emotions, David Seamands, Victor

The Twelve Steps—A Spiritual Journey, Recovery (workbook)

Twelve Steps for Christians, Recovery

Sin: Overcoming the Ultimate Deadly Addiction, Keith Miller

Love Is a Choice, Frank B. Minirth and Paul D. Meier, Thomas Nelson

The Pleasers, Kevin Leman, Dell

Getting Them Sober, vols. 1, 2, 3, Toby Rice Drews, Bridge

Intervention, Vernon E. Johnson, Johnson Inst.

I'll Quit Tomorrow, Vernon E. Johnson, Harper San Francisco

Dying for a Drink, Anderson Spickard and Barbara R. Thompson, Word

Facing Codependency, Pia Mellody et al., Harper San Francisco

Cutting Loose, Howard M. Halpern, Fireside (Simon & Schuster Trade); also Bantam (1989 ed.)

Hospitality Volunteers for Newcomers

Welcoming Newcomers

Thank you for volunteering to help us welcome visitors to (Northwest Bible Church). The interest visitors have in returning to (Northwest) is very often heavily influenced by their perception of our concern for them and willingness to reach out to them. A friendly phone call during the week after their Sunday visit to (Northwest) is a very important way of saying, "You are special to us!" With this letter, I am also giving you a packet of information to help you answer any questions that may arise during your phone conversations. I will use a rotation system for asking you to call, so you may hear from me only every month or so.

Following are a few suggestions to help you make your calls more meaningful. Remember that these are just suggestions; use your own words and feel free to add or take away from what I have listed.

Please make it a priority to call those on your list as soon as possible. Calling soon after their visit conveys that they are a priority to us and also gives us the opportunity to answer visitors' questions when they are still clear in their minds. I will try to get the names in the mail to you the day I receive them.

Again, thank you for your willingness to help in this important ministry. Please direct questions, problems, or any positive/negative comments gathered during your phone conversation to me (Name and phone number of coordinator).

1. Begin by introducing yourself, saying that you are from (Northwest Bible Church) and asking, "Have I caught you at a time that you can talk for a few minutes?" If not, call back at a more convenient time.
2. Express appreciation for their visit; in your own way, let them know that you are glad that they joined us on Sunday, e.g., "We're glad that you came to (NWBC) last Sunday."
3. All visitors are sent a letter from the pastor, and they are usually called by another staff pastor, who explains general church information and answers questions. The names that are sent to you are only those of women who live in the (Dallas) area, because our primary reason for calling is to provide additional information about Women's Ministries and to extend an invitation to join us. Ask, "Are you aware of our Women's Ministries program, which provides a Bible study followed by special elective classes on Tuesday mornings or Wednesday evenings? Would you like more information about it?"
4. It is possible that a staff member may not have contacted them, so they may have additional questions about the church. Feel free to answer any questions in this area. You may ask, "Can I answer any questions about our church for you?" If the answer is "No" or "Not really," you might proceed with a few more direct questions, e.g., "Were you able to find your way around all right?" "Do you have any questions about the Sunday school classes?" You might ask, "Did you have any trouble finding a parking place?" The Parking Posse will direct them to a special visitors' parking area if they are aware that the person is a visitor. If they did have trouble parking, suggest that they tell a member of the Parking Posse that they are visiting, if they choose to visit again. You might also ask, "Are you aware of the Wednesday night programs for children and adults that begin with a dinner at 5:15 P.M.?"

Suggestions for Hospital Visitation

1. Please call the patient before the visit to decide on a convenient time.
2. It is not necessary to take gifts, but a pretty card, a simple flower, or inspirational reading material would be nice (*Guideposts, Daily Walk,* or *Daily Bread*). Tapes may be borrowed from the church and picked up on your next visit (Sunday's sermon, Christian music).
3. Please don't visit when you are feeling "down"; the patient usually needs an uplifting experience. Being a good listener is very important, as the woman you are calling on may wish to talk.
4. Make note of any special needs of the person, such as requests for communion or a pastoral visit. Will there be a need for future visits from you when the patient goes home, or would an occasional phone call be sufficient?
5. You may wish to ask the following:
   a. "Is there anything I can do for you, such as write a note or run an errand?"
   b. "Is there any Bible passage that has a special meaning for you that I could read or that we could read together?" (Psalm 21; Philippians 4:6-7).
   c. "May we pray before I go?" A very short prayer is fine.
6. Please keep your visits short, perhaps just 3-5 minutes, with 15 minutes the maximum, unless the patient asks that you stay longer.
7. Please call the coordinator (phone) after each hospital visit, so that she can keep a record of who has been seen and can pass along any special needs that the patient has.
8. If you are visiting someone who has returned home from the hospital, you might remember the casseroles available in the freezer at the church.
9. We will try to have occasional meetings of our visitation committee, so that we may share helpful suggestions with each other. Please feel free to recommend books, pamphlets, or favorite Scripture to enable all of us to be more effective witnesses for Christ.

Tutoring in an Inner-city High School

The women at Northwest Bible Church have long been involved in West Dallas, an inner-city public housing community. Women have participated in various capacities through a local church's ministries. Most recently a concentrated effort has been made in a tutoring program for the public high school.

By meeting with the school's principal, permission was granted enthusiastically for us to begin a tutoring program that would pair women with one or two students. Offered as one of the electives in the weekly Women's Ministries program, the women carpooled to the high school and met with their students for approximately 35 minutes. Our providing a nursery and going as an organized group enabled many more women to participate.

The students volunteered for the program and seemed to need encouragement more than heavy academic tutoring. After the students returned to their classes, each session was closed with a prayer time The experience encouraged some women to tutor for a longer length of time on another day of the week.

God honored the commitment of the women in tremendous ways. By being faithful every week, the school officials and students knew it was *God's* love that motivated the women. Special relationships were made as only God could ordain, and women who had never seen the community before became burdened for the families who lived there to experience God's love and healing in their lives. The women saw answered prayers and a school welcoming their participation.

The only requirement is a willingness to serve God and flexibility in doing so.

Appendix 5
A Sample of Women's Ministries Brochures and Fliers

NORTHWEST BIBLE CHURCH

WOMEN'S MINISTRIES

Spring Session, 1992

God's Power For Our Inadequacy
The Life of Moses

Vickie Kraft
Bible Teacher

*Tuesday Morning
March 24-May 12
9:30-12:00 Program
10 minute fellowship break between
Bible Study and Electives
Wednesday Evening March 25-May 13
6:45-8:30 p.m.*

WEDNESDAY EVENING

Elective #C Current Issues for the Working Woman
A study based on the book Your Work Matters to God, by William Hendricks and Doug Sherman. Work dominates the landscape of modern life but unless you can connect what you do all day with what you think God wants you to be doing, you will never find ultimate meaning in either your work or your relationship with God. It starts with a certainty that "your work matters to God".
Leader: JoJo White

Elective #D Bible Study Discussion
Please join us for an in-depth study of the Bible lesson. This elective will provide a structured setting for probing of the Scriptures, for applying God's Word, and for keeping each other accountable.
Leader: Bobbi Wignall

Elective #E The Finishing Touch
Do you have any unfinished projects—your needlework or recipe files, photo albums, thank-you notes, etc.? Join other women and pursue your projects while you share, pray, encourage and enjoy each other's company.
Leader: Daphne Emslie

Elective #F Search for Significance
Most everyone yearns to feel worthwhile, but instead of pursuing the typical wrong goals, this class will focus on the biblical approach to finding significance. We will use the workbook by McGee.
Leader: Angela Adams   Limit:10

Elective #G Rubber Stamping
Come and learn the basics of how to use rubber stamps, plus how to emboss, make pop-up cards and other clever techniques. Something new every week.
Leader: Suzy Robb   Material Costs: $10

Spring Session Registration

Name _____

Address _____

City & Zip _____

Phone _____

Church Home _____

Class Choices: *List 2nd and 3rd choice*

_____ Tuesday Morning   _____ Wednesday Evening

1st _____

2nd _____

3rd _____

Tuesday Morning Children's Program
*Birth through Kindergarten, indicate birthdate
Reservations must be made for childcare*

Name _____ Birthdate _____

Name _____ Birthdate _____

Name _____ Birthdate _____

Return to the registration tables or mail to:
Vickie Kraft, Northwest Bible Church,
8505 Douglas, Dallas, 75225.

For Those Attending Bible Study, The Following Groups Are Available ...

WOMEN'S MINISTRIES

Elective #1 Vacation Bible School Workshop

A great way to help with summer VBS-planning, praying, and making nametags and decorations. Helpers of all ages and talents welcome. This year's theme is "Jesus is Our King", and children will be meeting Jesus as they hear the parables.
Leader: Mary Flo Ridley

Elective #2 Rubber Stamping

Come and learn the basics of how to use rubber stamps, plus how to emboss, make pop-up cards and other clever techniques. Something new every week.
Leader: Suzy Robb   Material Fees: $10

Elective #3 Homework Assistance at Pinkston High School

If you are interested in missions, but say "Please don't make me go to a foreign country!", come to West Dallas to assist high school students with their homework and prepare them for major exams. No expertise required. Training included in the first session. Carpool from church at 10:45, return by 12:15.
Leader: Joy Beless and Carroll Turpin

Elective #4 Potpourri of Cooking

Join us for a variety of culinary delights, ranging from appetizers to desserts, healthy and gourmet. Enjoy learning how to prepare the specialties of different cooks and enjoy tasting them, too, of course.
Leader: Glad Ramirez   Cost: $12.00

Elective #5 Bible Study Discussion

Please join us for an in-depth study of the Bible lesson. This elective will provide a structured setting for probing of the Scriptures, for applying God's Word, and for keeping each other accountable.
Leader: Pat Mooty

Elective #6 The Finishing Touch

Do you have any unfinished projects—needlework or recipe files, photo albums, thank-you notes, etc.? Join other women and pursue your projects while you share, pray, encourage and enjoy each other's company.
Leader: Marlyss Skipwith

Elective #7 Originally Yours

Who says you can't paint shirts like the pros?! We have Cricket by the Creek short sleeve shirts ready for your signature, and if the paint lasts, try your luck on tennis shoes, sunglasses and bathing suit cover-ups. It's fun, food, fellowship and art.
Leaders: Carol Cox and Pam Nesmith   Cost: $15

Elective #8 Nutrition's Focus

A practical and healthy approach to nutrition including nutrient and energy needs, cholesterol and fat recommendations for children and adults. We'll also discuss guidelines for establishing healthy eating behavior in children and dealing with those picky eaters, lowfat cooking, recipes, and eating out.
Leader: Paula Nyman, R.D., L.D.

Elective #9 The Austrian Craft Connection

"We Can Do it!" Perhaps you are not called to foreign missions, but you CAN contribute some crafts and handwork for our missionaries, which they can use in their ministry. Join us for fellowship, fun, craft making and prayer.
Leader: Shirley Rogers

Elective #10 Let's Make a Memory/Tradition

Join us and hear a different speaker each week share their established family memories/traditions concerning the different holidays, family activities, food, decorations and ideas that teach the joy and fun of being part of a Christian family.
Leader: Pat Humphrey

Elective #11 Learn to Teach a Bible Study

A class for those who feel motivated to teach biblical truths to others. We will look at the principles of communication and practice how to deliver a message effectively. Come learn and practice the valuable art of teaching others God's truth.
Leader: Lynna Lawrence   Limit: 10

Elective #A Home Schooling

We will explore the ups/downs and ins/outs of home schooling. This class will be aimed at those considering home schooling for the first time, but anyone interested may come.
Leaders: Beth Pattillo, Bonnie Dettmer

Elective #B Beginning with Christ

This class is for those people interested in a brand new relationship with Christ and those who want the practical steps to living the Christian life, i.e. reading the Bible and praying.
Leader: Sue Farr

**More Wednesday Evening
On Reverse Side**

WOMEN'S MINISTRIES SATURDAY SPECIAL
JULY SATURDAY SPECIAL
July 11th
Speaker: Alicia McNairy
"Seeking the Wisdom of God"
9:15-2:00 Bring a sack lunch
Nursery by reservations only (Bring lunch for children)

ELECTIVES:

Elective #A Beads, Beads, Beads

There are lots of fun things you can do with beads. Join us to make button covers & earrings. Then let your imagination run wild. Requires no talent.
Leaders: Pat Mills, Carol Cox Cost: $6.00

Elective #B Child Rearing

Opportunities for mothers of young children to talk about training, discipline, and problems of rearing children in a biblical manner.
Leader: Norma Kennedy

Elective #C Garage Sales

Stretch your decorating dollars by shopping at garage sales and outlets. Share special bargains with the group.
Leader: Jean Ann Bristol

Elective #D Rubber Stamping

Come learn the basics of rubber stamping and much, much more. We'll be making birthday cards.
Leader: Suzy Robb Limit: 15 Cost: $4.00

_____

Name_____Phone_____

Elective_____2nd Choice_____

Nursery Reservations: Child_____Age_____

Child_____Age___ Child_____Age_____

Turn in reservations to the Women's Ministries Office, Northwest Bible Church

Women's Ministries Service Opportunities

Welcoming Newcomers to NBC

This ministry consists of simply calling, welcoming, offering information, and answering questions about our church to women to visit.

_____ Yes, I'd like to welcome newcomers.

Name _____ Phone number _____

The Crisis Pregnancy Center

Are you interested in having a direct impact on the fight against abortion? Become a volunteer at the Crisis Pregnancy Center. Volunteers answer the hotline in their home or counsel women who come to the center. They inform them about the truth of abortion and have an opportunity to tell them of God's love for them. Volunteer counselor training is given. CPC also needs baby furnishings and maternity clothes. Contact: (Name and number)

_____ I'd like more information before I make a decision

_____ I'd like to investigate

_____ Volunteering as a counselor about 4 hours a week with training (a desperate need currently)

_____ Opening my home to an unwed mother

_____ Donating maternity clothes, infant clothes, equipment

_____ Baby-sitting for the children of volunteers in my home so others can be counselors

Name _____ Phone number _____

R.E.A.C.H.

This ministry reaches out to women facing crisis pregnancy. Once a woman chooses to give birth rather than have an abortion she has both practical needs as well as spiritual. R.E.A.C.H. volunteers offer encouragement and support throughout the pregnancy.

_____ I'd like more information on R.E.A.C.H. before I make a decision on involvement.

_____ Yes, I'd like to join the R.E.A.C.H. team and contribute what and when I can.

Name _____ Phone number _____

Women's Ministries Bulletin Board

_____ I would be willing to keep the bulletin board updated and see that it gets properly placed on Tuesday mornings.

Name _____ Phone number _____

Missions Projects

At the end of each session, the teaching tapes are sent to our women missionaries. Other areas of outreach to our women missionaries will be explored this year.

_____ Yes, I could help prepare and address the tapes for mailing.

_____ Yes, I'd like to be involved in exploring other ways we can encourage our missionaries. Here's an idea I have _____

_____

Name _____ Phone number _____

- -

Hospital Visitation

"I was sick and you visited me" (Matthew 25:36). Show the women of Northwest the love of Christ by visiting them in the hospital or later at home. Guidelines and helps provided. Contact: (Name and number)

_____ Yes, I'd be willing to make hospital visits.

_____ I'd like more information before I decide.

_____ Yes, I'd do this if I could go with another person.

Name _____ Phone number _____

- -

New Mother Visitation

Like babies? Join the team that visits new mothers in the hospital or in their homes. Call it a labor of love and encouragement. Contact: (Name and number)

_____ Yes, this sounds like fun. I'll try it!

Name _____ Phone number _____

- -

West Dallas Ministry

NBC helped found and continues to support the West Dallas Community Church, pastored by Aarvel Wilson. He and his wife, Eletha, not only minister to the community's spiritual needs but reach out in all the areas listed below and *more*. In what area can you help? No experience needed in any area, only a caring heart. Contact: (Name and number) or (Name and number)

I would like to learn more about and/or become involved in:

_____ Tutoring 1-2 times a week in the 1st, 2d or 3d grades at Carver Elementary School.

_____ Tutoring students at Pinkston High School in a room set apart especially for NBC to help them prepare for the TEAMS test to graduate.

_____ Helping call Pinkston High parents when children miss school.

_____ Helping with some of the 32 freshmen at Pinkston involved in the "I Have a Dream" program.

_____ Helping at West Dallas Church once or twice a week with adults and young people to help them pass the GED test.

_____ Doing something of my choice at the Senior Citizens Center such as setting up and showing one of the many videos from our church library or the *Jesus* film, performing music, helping with a craft, games or visiting.

_____ Spending time with young mothers who need some knowledge in caring for their babies and basic living skills for themselves.

Name _____ Phone number _____

Help in Church Office

When our church office has special projects or large mailings that could use extra hands, would you come to help and have fellowship with our secretarial staff and other volunteers while stuffing envelopes, etc.?

_____ I could help on a regular basis

_____ One day a week, *Which day?* _____

_____ One day a month, *Prefer* _____

_____ Place my name on a list to be called. I'll help when I am available.

Name _____ Phone number _____

Donations for Church Nursery

_____ I can donate good, used children's clothes (birth to 6 years) to be given to (1) our missionary families, (2) our church families, (3) West Dallas Church.

_____ I can make/donate doll clothes

_____ I can donate doll bedding

Name _____ Phone number _____

Dallas Life Foundation

This is a shelter that houses, feeds, and offers clothing to many homeless in Dallas. It is located near Old City Park.

I'd like to know more about:

_____ Leading or helping with a Bible study for women

      _____ On Monday evenings   _____ During the day

_____ Teaching or helping with a class on caring for and disciplining children from newborn to 6 years.

_____ Offering or helping with a craft type class to foster women-to-woman fellowship and encouragement.

_____ Arranging or helping with an outing to the zoo or a museum or other free activities for DLF residents.

_____ Teaching a 1-4 week class such as cooking for one, cooking in a crock pot, nutrition.

_____ Donating a _____, _____, _____.

Name _____ Phone number _____

Exploring New Ministries

Widows' Support Group

Women who have experienced the loss of their husbands will be able to minister to those who are suffering the same loss. This ministry will be for encouragement and fellowship.

_____ Yes, I would work with other interested women to start this group.

_____ Someone I know who might be interested in this group, _____.

Name _____ Phone number _____

Ministry to Nursing Homes

_____ I would like to be involved in ministering in nursing homes.

_____ I could serve in the following ways:

_____

_____

Name _____ Phone number _____

- -

Adopt a Grandparent

A family who is far away from their own parents may wish to reach out to a senior citizen in our body who has no family or who is living far away from his or her family. Both sides could be enriched from these relationships.

_____ Yes, I'd like to Adopt a Grandparent

_____ I'd like some family to adopt me as their grandparent

_____ I'd like to help facilitate such a program

Name _____ Phone number _____

- -

Support Group for Parents of Children with Special Needs

(Name) teaches a special Sunday School Class at 11:00 on Sunday mornings for children with special needs at NBC.

_____ I would like to help get such a support group started.

Name _____ Phone number _____

- -

Suggestions or Questions

_____

_____

_____

_____

_____

_____

_____

_____

_____

Name _____ Phone number _____

Notes

Other Helpful Resources for Women from Moody Press-

A Quiet Place of Rest

Finding Intimacy with God through a Daily Devotional Life

Quiet time. Daily devotions. Whatever you call them, our daily time alone with the Lord is essential for maintaining intimacy with Him. *A Place of Quiet Rest* actually teaches us **how** to have a rich, consistent devotional life. Speaking to the unique challenges women face, this book will encourage and refresh your time with God.

ISBN: 0-8024-6643-5 , Paperback

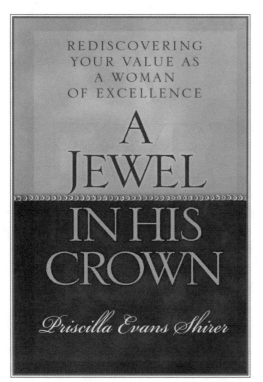

A Jewel in His Crown

Rediscovering Your Value as a Woman of Excellence

When they become weary and lose heart and discouraged, woman lose sight of their real value as beloved daughters of God. A Jewel in His Crown focuses on woman's self-esteem and how it deeply affects relationships. This book teaches woman how to renew their strength and become women of excellence.

ISBN: 0-8024-4097-5 , Paperback

MOODY
The Name You Can Trust
1-800-678-8812 www.MoodyPress.org

Other Helpful Resources for Women from Moody Press-

Releasing Your Potential

Using Your Gifts in a Thriving Women's Ministry

God can do amazing things in our churches when godly women are released to reach their spiritual potential, according to author and woman's leader Elizabeth Inrig. In Release Your Potential Inrig describes the path to achieving a strong, dynamic ministry among women in the local church. She gives practical answers to questions like, "How can we build a thriving, productive women's ministry?" and "What kind of women does the church need?" So, what kind of women do churches need?

ISBN: 0-8024-8498-0 , Paperback

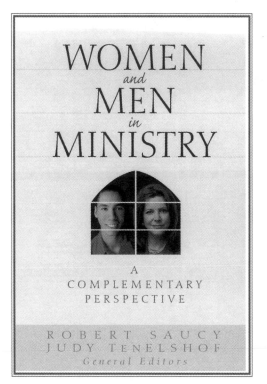

Women and Men in Ministry

A Complementary Perspective

Women and Men were created to complement each other, and the church functions best when they minister in a complementary fashion. Using a variety of approaches, from a study of relevant Scriptures to a look at cultural patterns, *Women and Men in Ministry* focuses on our unity as equals and on the importance of a church's using separate gender strengths in a complementary way.

"A Godly relationship between men and women in the church is indispensible to it's witness in the world."

ISBN: 0-8024-5291-4 , Paperback

MOODY
The Name You Can Trust
1-800-678-8812 www.MoodyPress.org

Moody Press, a ministry of Moody Bible Institute,
is designed for education, evangelization, and edification.
If we may assist you in knowing more about Christ
and the Christian life, please write us without obligation.
Moody Press, c/o MLM, Chicago, Illinois 60610.